praise for
the practice of belonging

"Building sustainable justice in the world requires telescoping from the personal to the interpersonal to the systemic with such frequency it can feel impossible. What a gift that *The Practice of Belonging* helps us do exactly that in ways that become fluid and even joy filled instead of terrifying. Kentgen's book put me in mind of Leah Lakshmi Piepzna-Samarasinha's book *Care Work,* and . . . gives me hope for the possibility of communities that aren't only just but are also delightful."

—SANDHYA JHA, activist and author of *Transforming Communities*

"*The Practice of Belonging* is a uniquely powerful book. The author speaks profoundly of community's meaning and tells us where this possibility is occurring in the world right now . . . making the world we want to inhabit accessible to us. The insight of one chapter title, 'The Vulnerable Help Us Shed Our Masks,' is reason enough to embrace this book. There is a quiet and essentially unreported movement occurring in our local places, and this book and the way it is written hasten this along."

—PETER BLOCK, author of *Community*

"This book is a powerful master class in how to set up vibrant communities at a time when connecting with each other has never been more important. We have a choice about the cultures we build. *The Practice of Belonging* offers a first-of-its-kind road map to build cultures of belonging, inclusion, and support so that we thrive."

—BETHANY KLYNN, organizational psychologist and president of
Insight Leadership Consulting

"Given our current climate of political and social divide, *The Practice of Belonging* could not come at a more needed time. Dr. Kentgen explores how we can solve our crisis of belonging and heal our unprecedented social and emotional pain. While traveling across the country and meeting with people who shared their experiences of their healthy communities, she discovered six qualities that all vibrant communities share and invites us to use these same qualities to build our own shared spaces of healthy belonging."

—DEBRA A. HARKINS, professor of sociology and criminal justice at Suffolk University and author of *Alongside Community*

"In this passionate book about vibrant community, Kentgen takes the reader on an unforgettable tour of sanctuaries where mutual care and the commitment to a shared way of life are alive and thriving. Heartful, intelligent, and deeply inspiring, this journey to visit the front lines of the 'belonging revolution'—and to meet the extraordinary people who are making it happen—offers hope and vision for a more communal future. A *cri de coeur* against the epidemic of loneliness overwhelming our nation. I highly recommend it."

—MARK MATOUSEK, author of *Ethical Wisdom*

"*The Practice of Belonging* is nourishment for the weary spirit. In a time of intensifying polarization, Dr. Kentgen's book offers an accessible way to explore what it means to cultivate community and togetherness. Drawing on the collective expertise of vibrant communities across the United States, this book is a poignant reminder that relationships matter, and that we have the power to cultivate vibrancy in any community we belong to."

—KARI GRAIN, PhD, author of *Critical Hope*

the
practice
of
belonging

**six lessons from
vibrant communities
to combat loneliness,
foster diversity,
and cultivate caring
relationships**

lisa kentgen, ph.d.

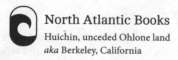

North Atlantic Books
Huichin, unceded Ohlone land
aka Berkeley, California

Published by
North Atlantic Books
Huichin, unceded Ohlone land
aka Berkeley, California

Cover design by Jasmine Hromjak
Book design by Happenstance Type-O-Rama

Printed in the United States of America

The Practice of Belonging: Six Lessons from Vibrant Communities to Combat Loneliness, Foster Diversity, and Cultivate Caring Relationships is sponsored and published by North Atlantic Books, an educational nonprofit based in the unceded Ohlone land Huichin (*aka* Berkeley, California) that collaborates with partners to develop cross-cultural perspectives; nurture holistic views of art, science, the humanities, and healing; and seed personal and global transformation by publishing work on the relationship of body, spirit, and nature.

North Atlantic Books' publications are distributed to the US trade and internationally by Penguin Random House Publisher Services. For further information, visit our website at www.northatlanticbooks.com.

Library of Congress Cataloging-in-Publication Data

Names: Kentgen, Lisa, author.
Title: The practice of belonging : six lessons from vibrant communities to combat loneliness, foster diversity, and cultivate caring relationships / Lisa Kentgen.
Description: Huichin, unceded Ohlone land aka Berkeley, California : North Atlantic Books, [2023] | Includes index. | Summary: "Kentgen explores the ways in which we as a society experience isolation and its effects on our mental and physical healths; she proceeds to offer solutions in order to collectively work towards building a sense of authentic belonging and communication in six specific ways"— Provided by publisher.
Identifiers: LCCN 2022032450 (print) | LCCN 2022032451 (ebook) | ISBN 9781623177638 (trade paperback) | ISBN 9781623177645 (ebook)
Subjects: LCSH: Social isolation. | Belonging (Social psychology) | Loneliness.
Classification: LCC HM1131 .K46 2022 (print) | LCC HM1131 (ebook) | DDC 302.5/45—dc23/eng/20220720
LC record available at https://lccn.loc.gov/2022032450
LC ebook record available at https://lccn.loc.gov/2022032451

1 2 3 4 5 6 7 8 9 KPC 27 26 25 24 23

contents

acknowledgments

Above all else, this book was made possible by the generosity of so many people who offered their time and insights, some of whom have been creating community for years and others who are more recent converts. I'm inspired by every person who offered a window into what building, strengthening, and deepening communities look like.

From Harmony Project, many thanks to Roni Burkes-Trowsdell, David Brown, Reggie Jackson, Melissa Gavin-Smith, and Kadi McDonald, who showed me hospitality when I visited Columbus, Ohio, and afterward. Gratitude to people at Community First! Village, including Ute Dittemer, Mike Walker, Alan Graham, and Haley Maresh, who offered valuable insights into what turns a village of tiny homes into a community of caring individuals. I am indebted to people from the L'Arche community—Tina Bovermann, Laurie Pippenger, Bruce Weaver, Charles Clark, Francene Short, Luke Smith, Curt Armstrong, Ben Nolan, and Sarah Moore. Within the dharma community, thanks go to DaRa Williams, Carol Cano, Rebecca Bradshaw, and Lynn Whittemore. Vince Two Eagles, Amy Doom, Margaret Zephier, Parker Palmer, John Fenner, Richard Shugerman, and Donna Bivens graciously shared their wisdom on holding tension, handling conflict, and skillfully communicating across differences. Thanks to Jennifer Rose Marie Serna at Wapato Island Farm and Adam Greenfield of Playwrights Horizons. Other people who shared are Tim League, Kortney Lawlor, Malcolm Shabazz Hoover, Mirabai Collins, Anita Garcia Morales, Tom Brackett, Jason Ikpatt, Barbara Poppe, and Ross Gay. To every person over the past several years who said "yes" to conversation around community, thank you. Every encounter sowed seeds and made an impact, regardless of whether it made it into these pages.

Therese Arkenberg offered wise guidance, micro and macro, throughout the entire process, getting the first look at every chapter as it was written—I am grateful. Meredith Tennant was helpful in editing an earlier version of the manuscript. And thanks to Shayna Keyles at North Atlantic Books for her interest and support in bringing *The Practice of Belonging* into the world.

For my dear ones whose expressions of care and love are an internalized buoy that lifts me up and connects me to the beauty in this world. And, of course, to you, the reader—it's my privilege to join you for a short time on your own path to creating a better world, one where we lead from the heart and place relationship first.

introduction:
a crisis in belonging

Melissa could never have imagined her successful life—having a meaningful full-time job, with good benefits, and people who love and respect her. She values giving back, especially when she can inspire others to believe that change is possible, for everyone, at any time. Melissa also has the relatively new experience of feeling pride in her accomplishments. Yet she knows she wouldn't be here without the support and care of others.

Today, Melissa places a high value on being intentional in all her relationships, mindful of how her words, choices, and actions impact others. She admires people within her communities who have been intentional in their interactions with her, a quality that built trust between them.

She works at a probate court, where she interfaces with hundreds of people daily by phone and in person. "When people are coming to probate court, 90 percent of the time there is a sad story behind it," she said. She performs her job with compassion and has a perspective that is a little different from her coworkers.

Growing up, Melissa learned important life lessons from her mother, such as acceptance, nonjudgment, and caring for others. But she didn't have access to people who could model how to succeed in life in terms of supporting herself and her family. Finding that would wait until she discovered community while she was incarcerated.

Two of Melissa's favorite things to talk about are the Harmony Project and the Tapestry program, the two communities responsible for helping her turn her life around. She encountered both as an inmate in the Ohio Reformatory for Women in Marysville, Ohio, just outside Columbus.

The first eighteen months of her three-year sentence were spent in the Tapestry program, a unique therapeutic community of eighty women within the larger prison. There, Melissa received intensive behavior therapy for her recovery, as well as other educational opportunities. She was surrounded by her "sisters," other women in the program, who were a powerful source of support and acceptance. This community helped her through the darkest times, when guilt and remorse just about killed her, by letting her know she was not alone.

Women in the Tapestry program have the opportunity to participate in the Inside Out Choir, part of the Harmony Project in Columbus. According to Melissa, when the Harmony volunteers enter the facility for weekly choir practice, they usher in a big wave of energy and love. "David [Brown, the choir director] brings twenty-five other people, and you can tell by their body language, how they look at and talk to you, that they genuinely care."

After she graduated from the Tapestry program, she returned weekly as an alumna to participate in the choir, also serving as a model for other women there. As her release date neared, Melissa knew it was not in her best interests to leave the halfway house where she was living and return to Newark, Ohio, where she'd lived at the time of her arrest. "They like to send you back to your county where you were charged, which is not supportive," she explained. She went to her unit manager and said, "I can't go back to Newark. The people I met are all in Columbus. I want to go there and be part of the Harmony Project program."

She recalls a pivotal moment from that time: "I can remember a conversation I had with David a few months before my release about my wanting to come to Columbus. He assured me, 'You come to Columbus, Melissa. You don't have to worry. We will make sure that you are good.'" Roni Burkes-Trowsdell, another choir member, supported Melissa's decision to land in Columbus. This carried weight because Roni was the warden of the Ohio Reformatory for Women and the person who had partnered with David to bring Harmony into the prison.

The first phone call Melissa made when she was free was to Harmony. After being released with no money or street clothes, eight days later she attended choir practice.

Melissa remembers her fear when she arrived at that first choir practice as a free woman. "I got there super early and immediately felt the love. David and Shelby [the office manager] took me into the office, instead of making me go to the choir space by myself, and we began building connections just then.

"And when it was time to go to choir practice, Shelby locked arms with mine and said, 'C'mon, Melissa.'" They walked into the choir space and Melissa was enveloped in tears, hugs, and love. They weren't just any kind of hug, but the kind she wasn't allowed to have in prison, a thirty-second healing hug "where you feel someone else's heart beating next to yours." (Melissa says Tapestry is different from the rest of the correctional facility in that hugs are allowed, but they must be brief.)

Melissa read me a beautiful poem she had written and read during a Harmony concert in the Ohio Theatre to an audience of over five thousand people. The poem included these words:

> I'm stuck daily,
> daydreaming and wondering
> if I'll ever be the "me" I deserve to be. . . .
> Now I'm here and it's changing.
> Sober, determined, loved, amazing.
> I'm still so shocked by the changes going on inside of me.
> Living healthy is like being in a dream.

The Harmony Project, through music and volunteer service, meaningfully connects people who otherwise wouldn't cross paths. In 2009, Harmony began as a single choir of one hundred people, none of whom were required to audition. Since then, thousands of people have participated in its choirs, programs, and service projects. And many thousands of people have sat in the audience of its biannual concerts. You'll read more about this choir in chapter 1.

David, the choir's director, laments all the ways in which we are separated from each other. "What I believe we're doing here in Harmony is finding new ways to live together," he says. "We're focusing on what connects us beyond the fact that we're going to vote differently, pray differently, and live and love differently."

Belonging Is an Essential Human Need

This book is about belonging, which is a central issue of our time. It is a call to stretch our conception of connection and to strengthen the "we" muscle that has atrophied. Our collective health and the sustainability of the planet require a shift of focus toward relating to each other in fundamentally different ways.

The experience of belonging is essential for physical health, emotional well-being, and the ability to do well in life. A meta-analysis that looked at nearly 150 smaller studies with over three hundred thousand participants within the studies found that a sense of belonging had a positive health impact as powerful as quitting smoking, diet, and exercise combined![1] Whatever a person's age or particular life circumstances, they will live healthier and longer if they have a sense of belonging.

When children experience belonging in school, they are better able to proactively shape their lives later on.[2] The number one influence on how teenagers perform in high school is whether they feel they fit in.[3] What kids take away from their entire school experience, and how it prepares them for adulthood, has more to do with whether they find a social home than all the effort that goes into educating them. If we take this seriously, then every educational system's priority should be creating an atmosphere of safety and belonging.

The importance of belonging is not fully appreciated, and we are currently in a crisis of connection that has catastrophic consequences. Though this crisis is not new, we are witnessing its effects more clearly than ever before. A 2018 survey of twenty thousand adults found that nearly half of those who responded felt lonely and did not have meaningful social interactions on most days.[4]

This crisis of belonging is reflected in high rates of depression among people of all ages, with the highest increases seen in young people and the elderly.[5] This crisis is sometimes referred to as a loneliness epidemic. Loneliness is a state of mind in which people feel alone, empty, and unwanted. Even when other people are around, loneliness leaves us experiencing ourselves as disconnected and separate.

Loneliness is linked with poor mental and physical health, and like depression, it is growing the most in youth[6] and older people.[7] It puts people at risk for a whole range of health problems, including alcohol abuse and other forms of substance abuse. And the ways in which people try to cope with feeling separate, such as numbing the pain with substances, can then intensify the sense of aloneness. The general experience of separateness has only intensified since the onset of the COVID-19 epidemic in 2020, which left many to experience new forms of social isolation for prolonged periods. We are still adapting to this new form of separateness.

The plight of isolation impairs our ability to collectively care for ourselves and each other. The rise in loneliness parallels a rise of the extreme polarization that seems to be ever present in the United States. Although it is unclear if and how our national discord contributes to the loneliness crisis, what is certain is that it creates obstacles to caring for one another.

If we don't learn to belong to each other in healthier ways, the trajectory of isolation and harmful outcomes will continue. How do we distance ourselves from the unhealthy aspects of the culture in which we are immersed? An important first step is recognizing the ways in which our culture is transactional, promoting separateness and eroding solidarity. The next step is to examine how we personally participate—often inadvertently—in dynamics that diminish connection and mutual care.

The truth is that we also show care for each other every single day in both small gestures and large acts of kindness. But these stories get drowned out by the narrative of our separateness. The narrative changes when there are more places we can plug into where caring for each other is the primary story told in myriad ways. We need more models of relationship and connection that point the way to what is possible, what we can become, and what we already know how to do.

Revolutionary belonging is a call to foster our authentic voices and unique gifts, then use them in the service of others. It is an invitation to cultivate a perspective that focuses on the "we" over and above the "I," and to live from that place. We change course by first changing our priorities. True belonging is possible when we gather together in ways that place relationship at the forefront, and we practice compassionate communication with one another.

● ● ●

In the United States, the ways in which we gather have changed dramatically over the past fifty years. There has been a decades-long trend away from traditional forms of community where the same groups of people regularly met in person.[8] For example, whereas most people used to fulfill their need for spiritual affiliation within religious institutions and the communities around them, today more people are searching for more personal expressions of faith and values. And we socialize differently; we're now more likely to attend discrete events that appeal to us than to join social organizations or hang out with our neighbors. Community is still perceived as essential to our well-being, but for too many people it is an unmet or inadequately met need, and there is a longing for places where we are known and valued.

The shift away from traditional forms of gathering is not necessarily unhealthy, because many of those communities required members to fit into rigid roles or hold similar beliefs. Group cohesiveness was prioritized and protected, often at the expense of member authenticity. Those who were different had to hide aspects of themselves in order to fit in; the alternative was accepting the emotionally costly choice of personal growth along with nonacceptance by the group.

While the traditional forms of community have waned, there has been an increase in participation in activities that promote self-exploration, emotional wellness, and personal insight.[9] This is reflected in the popularity of books, courses, seminars, and retreats focused on personal growth.[10] Another important cultural development is the acceptance of psychotherapy, now seen as a sign of mental health rather than psychopathology.

These dual patterns—of less membership participation and greater personal exploration—are sometimes characterized as a shift toward a me-first mentality. But this is mistaken: people want to participate in something greater than themselves, but not at the cost of their individuality. Still, the decreased participation in traditional forms of community has left a hole in the web of social supports. Now we must cultivate our "we" muscle and find ways to bring our unique voices into more communal ways of living.

Individuality and Individualism

Individuality refers to the qualities that make you uniquely you. Parents, for example, support their child's individuality when they show curiosity about their child's beliefs and evolving identities that differ from their own. Individualism is a stance or philosophy that values individual freedom of action over the needs of the collective. Western countries that value individualism are likely to value independence, personal achievement, and competition over collective participation and collaboration. However, even in more traditionally collectivist cultures, such as China and Japan, support for collective values is decreasing among the young and wealthy.[11]

Individuality and communality are often viewed as inherently at odds, which is unfortunate because emphasizing contrasts in these ideas can turn people away from the life-enhancing benefits of community participation. The radical individualism we see in which the greatest premium is placed on individual achievement, unlike healthy individuality, weakens our basic sense of solidarity. Individualism, not tempered by a deep commitment to the collective, undermines the conditions of safety needed for true personal freedom and well-being.

Naturally, sometimes there is tension between the needs of the individual and those of the group. Healthy communities welcome the uniqueness of individuals, and the tension need not be fully resolved or experienced as conflict. To seed the ground for healthy belonging, communities need to support our individuality, which is the foundation for authenticity. We can be our unique selves within our communities while valuing being part of something greater than ourselves, refusing to buy into the kind of individualism that characterizes a lonely and divided culture.

● ● ●

The changing tides of how we gather now intersect with our transactional culture, which erects barriers to healthy belonging and authentic connection. In a transactional culture, our dignity and worth are contingent upon external measures of success, which can impede building deep and lasting relationships. Cooperation and collaboration are undervalued, and competition can manifest as an unhealthy near-obsession with winning. Healthy competition, in contrast, is an environment in which everyone strives to do their best while also celebrating the accomplishments of others. A mindset of healthy competition enables us to work hard and reach toward our goals, without viewing ourselves as above others to accomplish this. An inspiring example of healthy competition is when a runner stops during a race to help an injured rival cross the finish line.

The severity of the climate crisis has made the truth of our interconnectedness overwhelmingly clear, yet we can feel helpless when trying to imagine ways forward toward solutions when our differences seem irreconcilable. Only when we value collaboration and trust building over competition will we be in the best position to work together effectively to solve both local and global challenges.

We need a paradigm shift in which we build communities that cultivate the voices of unique individuals, who then bring the best of themselves to benefit the collective. These communities are places where there is an appreciation of difference, and where we work toward mutual goals that reflect shared core values. But to create them, there needs to be a real shift in how we personally spend our time, energy, and resources.

The good news is that we can learn the skills to build more communal ways of relating that will lead to a happier and healthier future. Getting there will require a perceptual shift and an all-out commitment to do our part to create that future—one where we prioritize the community without muting our authentic voices, socialize more communally, and consistently show up for our communities while still fulfilling our personal responsibilities.

A Revolution of the Heart

There are two questions at the heart of this book:

- What are the qualities of community that will help us transform the way we relate to each other?
- How do we bring the spirit of community to all our relationships, into our social lives and our workplaces?

We are at a juncture where we must face the necessity of learning to cooperate and care for each other on a scale that hasn't yet been done. Qualitative change happens incrementally, the result of small movements built up over time. Small movements toward change can lead to a critical tipping point that ushers in transformation, a radical shift in how we think and act. Such a transformation can happen in a time of intense discomfort or crisis, a time like the one we are now in.

Communities that develop in response to crises often end once the crisis is no longer at the forefront. But now there is greater awareness of the ways in which existing power structures are inherently unjust and are intended to reward some groups at the expense of others. If we cannot create the conditions to build communities where everyone can develop and offer up their gifts for the good of all, then we cannot address the crisis of separateness that harms us all. If we persist in our efforts, turning the yearning for belonging into a genuine movement, we can create the conditions for safety and connection for everyone.

The thirst for greater connection and strong community ties is real and strong, but a community-focused framework is still viewed as an alternate way of living. Many small movements have been growing for some time, but the sea change hasn't yet happened. We may be reaching a tipping point, as increasingly more people recognize that the way we are collectively relating to each other is unhealthy, and as they seek more connected ways of living. Yet we still need to develop and practice skills that will serve us in our communities.

We can move toward healthier methods of relating through the incubators of vibrant communities. They call us to slow down, live more simply, and pay better attention to each other. Being in a vibrant community lets us translate our yearnings for belonging into connections between each other. Vibrant community is also a state of mind, one where we find purpose in taking responsibility for each other's well-being.

The word *community* is like the word *love*: it means different things to different people and can be difficult to precisely define. The word is often used in ways that do not represent close, personal relationships between people. People generally believe that community is important, but they may be unclear about how it is different—or if it is different— from family, friends, and other social groups.

Community is defined here as the experience of solidarity and belonging with others who share values, interests, and experiences. *Vibrant* community is distinguished as a community that people consciously choose to join with the understanding that they are making a commitment to prioritize relationships with the people in it. Within vibrant communities, there is a preference to meet in person, consistently even if not frequently.

Communities at the heart of change are about connecting first as human beings and opening more fully to love. Whatever the community's mission and goals, relationships are the most important thing. Vibrant communities create and hold spaces of physical and emotional safety that enable authentic connection to evolve. This evolution is messy, inefficient, and imperfect. In vibrant communities, the skills of reciprocity, inclusion, and exchange are practiced. These skills guide us out of the crisis of separateness and toward a way of belonging that we have yet to collectively realize.

"When you bring very different people together, that contact reduces prejudice and changes attitudes," says Tina Bovermann, the national leader of L'Arche USA, a community you will meet in chapter 3. "This is the scientific answer of how change happens. But for me, when you meet 'the other,' with no goal other than relationship itself, then you have created the invitation and the safe space for something special to happen. That something is transformation. What happens in our community can happen anywhere. It is not a product; it is a platform."

In vibrant communities, the relationships within them are distinct from other social connections and even friendships, but they don't exclude other relationships. Although community members have shared values and experiences, those relationships aren't chosen in the same way as we choose our friends. In fact, communities formed among existing friends have a higher likelihood of breaking up because it is more challenging to relate to each other differently once relationships are established.[12]

Vital to any healthy community is building trust within relationships. This is why a commitment to show up regularly and in person is important. Vibrant communities work to create open and nonjudgmental spaces so that members can take off the masks they wear in the world and be vulnerable. In these places, we learn to speak up and to listen; we are accepted, and we practice acceptance.

Some people may prefer online communities to in-person ones, or they may have difficulty meeting in person because of time constraints or because their communities are geographically spread out. The differences between meeting in person, in close physical proximity, and meeting in online community will be explored in the first chapter, but it is not an either/or proposition. Practicing the skills of community building in person strengthens trust and bonds in all our communities, including our valued online ones.

· · ·

The research for this book consisted primarily of conversations with dozens of people about community, what it means to them, and how participating in it impacts their perspectives and lives. All the communities are in the United States with the exception of one in France (which has counterparts in the US). The intention was to visit all these places in person, but this was not always possible, especially after the arrival of COVID-19. I tried to choose communities that were diverse along different dimensions and that represented a wide variety of life experiences.

I use everyone's first and last names when I have had personal conversations with them, unless they prefer that I use only their first names. I use first names by themselves when I am referring to conversations held before I was doing research for this book, which thus predated my asking for permission.

The way those interviewed spoke about and participated in community varied, yet there were common themes across all the conversations. Some people you will meet belong to long-established and well-organized communities. Others are exploring new ways to make community central to their lives and joining with people who want the same. The willingness of so many to share their time and stories reflects how important community is to them, as well as the generous spirit of the people who are attracted to creating community.

They gather in cities, suburbs, and small towns. They show up for each other—eating, sharing stories, singing, working, making art, volunteering, meditating, creating rituals, and praying together. They find joy and meaning in each other's presence, and they struggle with each other. They prioritize relationship and have in common a desire to deepen the experience of community, believing that *I* am lifted up by *we*.

Communities you will meet include a choir of more than five hundred nonauditioned singers in Columbus, Ohio; a village of tiny homes for the most vulnerable in Austin, Texas; a worldwide community celebrating the gifts of people with cognitive disabilities; Native and non-Native people who created a first-of-its-kind dialogue on racism in South Dakota; Buddhist spiritual centers doing the hard work of breaking down barriers to inclusion; a women-run farm using folk herbalism and indigenous practices to build cultural resilience in Portland, Oregon; and an off-Broadway theater trying to return to its ancient roots as community ritual.

What Differentiates a Vibrant Community?

When I reflected upon the conversations and experiences I had with these communities, six qualities stood out that distinguished them from other types of groups and gatherings. These six qualities are the focus of the book, and they are what makes a community vibrant. If we prioritize these same qualities in our existing relationships, we can deepen the experience of belonging and transform how we relate to each other.

The first quality, explored in chapter 2, is an explicit commitment to care for each other, which is a universal attribute among all vibrant communities. This commitment nurtures a sense of belonging, which is a fundamental human need. This quality may seem obvious, but it is not explicit in most established groups and social gatherings; nor is it a given in personal relationships. As with all the six qualities, a commitment to care is a verb and not a noun, an active practice that is reflected in our perceptions, thoughts, choices, and actions. Melissa, whom you met earlier, has a practice of care reflected in her commitment to be thoughtful in how she speaks to others.

The other five qualities are valued in all vibrant communities and are practiced to some degree. I found that each community often embodied two or three of the qualities in unique and powerful ways.

The second quality of vibrant community is acceptance, valuing people for who they are, which is essential for fostering authenticity. When we are accepted, we don't have to hide aspects of ourselves, including things that embarrass us or that we experience as broken. Chapter 3 introduces you to a community that practices radical acceptance, and the members most skilled at community building have themselves known the pain of rejection.

The third quality is diversity, valuing it and recognizing that it strengthens the community. Although most vibrant communities welcome diversity and aspire to greater inclusion, they can have difficulty making it a reality. A diverse community cannot happen without making it an explicit priority of the entire group. This is especially true in a well-established community, where it is more difficult to make the kinds of changes needed for greater inclusion. Chapter 4 looks at why greater diversity can be so elusive and at strategies communities employ to successfully overcome these challenges.

The fourth quality is that vibrant communities have skillful ways to handle their differences that allow them to move beyond conflict toward understanding. Sometimes communities need the help of facilitators to structure the dialogue in ways that build trust so they can hold conversations around difficult topics. Chapter 5 offers a model of how groups with a history of conflict shaped their dialogues in order to facilitate solutions that create the possibility for future healing and reconciliation.

The fifth quality found in vibrant communities is the high value placed on celebration and ritual. Alongside sharing the mundane details of day-to-day life, these communities intentionally create opportunities for meaningful bonding and having fun. Ceremony and ritual are meaningful only *because* they take place within the context of caring relationships. Chapter 6 explores how ritual enables people to participate meaningfully in the experience of community.

And the sixth quality is the gift of hospitality, which is the art of welcoming guests. This attribute runs counter to the premium that our consumerist culture places on exclusivity. Vibrant communities put effort into finding creative ways for people outside their membership to meaningfully participate in the experience of community. Chapter 7 gives examples of the ways in which these communities balance extending hospitality to others with respecting their own boundaries.

It can't be emphasized enough that these six transformational qualities don't just happen—they are generated by us. As with anything in life that matters most, these qualities are fostered through intention. They take ongoing effort and, at times, very hard work.

What does it mean to put relationship first and to commit to caring for every member within our communities? What would it look like, concretely, to practice acceptance, both for others and ourselves? How can we create a climate of true inclusivity within our communities, one where our differences both challenge and strengthen us? How can we learn to feel more comfortable with tension and acquire the skills to move through conflict toward creative solutions? What would happen if we incorporated meaningful rituals into our communities and made a point of celebrating each other? And what if we again elevated the ancient virtue of hospitality, valuing guests and welcoming them into our lives?

Community is the most effective platform to cultivate these qualities. Developing practices around each of these qualities will teach us healthy belonging and will fundamentally transform how we relate to each other. The final chapter encourages us to extend the care we practice in our personal communities to those outside them, including the earth itself and all living things that sustain us.

* * *

A vibrant community can be created when just a few people come together for a shared purpose and commit to each other. It might look like reading and discussing a book, playing a game, meditating or praying, dancing and singing, telling stories, environmental activism, or a monthly invitation to a potluck dinner. What plants the seeds of vibrant community in any gathering is its explicit commitment to put relationship first and show up.

Some of the communities described in this book have grown substantially from when they first began and have developed organizational structures to support them. Some have a certain "wow" factor, a momentum and energy around the work they do that attract and inspire others from outside. None of these communities started out with an explicit goal of growing the way they have. But what makes them transformative is often not what attracts public attention; it is that they are designed to provide ample opportunity for personal connection between people. It is these personal connections, often between people who would not otherwise meet, where we can learn new ways of relating and belonging to each other.

We don't need tremendous resources or large numbers of people joining us to create community that is a positive force for change, both in our personal lives and in the world.

Instead of finding the kind of community to which we imagine ourselves belonging, the better approach is to start building community right now in small, meaningful ways. Toward that end, an important question to reflect upon is: How do I bring the qualities of vibrant community into all areas of my life?

How I Developed a Communal Lens

How do we cultivate in our communities a greater sense of belonging, so that people feel recognized and cared for, and that they matter? What is it about certain group experiences that bring out the best in us and make us feel part of something greater than ourselves? These questions have lingered with me over the years and became front and center in my awareness while writing this book.

As a psychologist, I have a deep appreciation for the power of psychotherapy to help people gain personal insight, accept themselves, get relief from painful symptoms, and acquire skills for healthy living. Yet even if every person had access to good therapy, this would not adequately address the crisis of belonging that harms our collective well-being. For that, we need communities of individuals with whom we can be authentic, share our lives, and participate in something greater than ourselves.

When I was a child and into my young adult years, my parents met regularly with four other couples. Their gatherings included some form of reflection or prayer, followed by sharing each other's lives—their joys, struggles, values, and aspirations. Though I had a web of other caring adults in my life, my connection to my parents' community felt a little different. I wonder if I vicariously experienced belonging as I saw it modeled in their commitment to each other and to me, as an extension of their community.

Looking back while writing this book, I developed a greater appreciation for some of the lessons my parents modeled around community and care. For example, when I was in grade school, a show band from Mexico, the Acapulco Loco, came to live in our Silver Eagle trailer behind the house for a few months after their housing plans unexpectedly fell through. The band had come to try to establish a following for themselves in the Chicagoland area. Salvador, their drummer, was engaged to Linda, whom I met when I was ten years old after returning her dog who had gotten loose. It didn't occur to me that my parents' hospitality might be seen as strange until my best friend told me my family was now a hot topic of conversation at the neighborhood coffee klatch. Fortunately, the neighbors accepted an invitation to an Acapulco Loco concert in our unfinished basement, where we danced and new kinds of stories were hatched for the next morning's coffee klatch.

Like most people, as an adult I've experienced different forms of community outside of family and friendships. Mine have included spiritual communities and those forged around a common purpose, such as protecting the environment. In general, though, these groups didn't have the explicit purpose of cultivating and strengthening bonds between the members of the community themselves. Still, within these spaces we came to care for each other because of our shared experience and natural inclination to connect. But this was different from intentionally and explicitly placing relationship front and center.

I've always valued community and my relationships, but in retrospect I understand that I used to see them as somewhat separate things or as fulfilling different purposes. I cared about everyone in my personal communities, and when deep friendships would sometimes develop, those people would then be in the categories of both friend and community member. It was only much later that I intuited how community is actually a container for all my relationships, including the natural world and people I've yet to meet. This shift in perception, where community is central, generates a deeper internal experience of belonging and connection regardless of what is happening around me.

I have never participated in a popular form of community called intentional community, where people who hold a common vision live under the same roof or in proximity. For example, ecovillages are intentional communities where people live together with a shared value of becoming sustainable and self-reliant. The interest in these kinds of community has burgeoned in the past decade or so. L'Arche, which you will meet in chapter 3, is a wonderful example of an intentional community.

For many people, living in an intentional community is not possible or compatible with their life choices and responsibilities. And yet communities like these, which share resources as a form of care, are important models from which we can learn. So while thinking about which communities to include in the book, I frequently asked myself which models of community offer the kinds of shared experiences similar to those of intentional community.

Experiencing the energy generated from so many enriching conversations led to the awareness that interacting with people who value and practice community enhances a personal sense of connection and belonging. When community becomes central in our lives, it is like a healing balm that helps us stay present and connected in a world that manifests, along with its beauty, the pain of our separateness.

The very act of focusing on the question "What is vibrant community?" for an extended period of time led to a personal awareness that it is within my power to foster such communities. Every one of us can. It is tremendously freeing to not wait and hope for conditions to change before accepting the invitation to practice and prioritize living in healthier connection. The transformation happens when we live in a community-oriented way in which we care for each other through it all—our joys and pains—and where people are encouraged to show who they authentically are, and everyone's unique contributions are considered necessary.

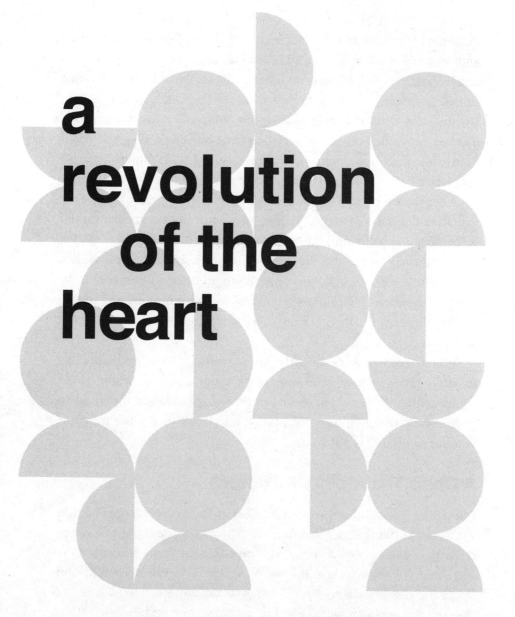

a revolution of the heart

Without community there is no liberation. . . . But
community must not mean shedding our differences,
nor the pretense that these differences do not exist.[1]

—AUDRE LORDE

Belonging is something that's not frequently the object of our reflection, and yet we have a deep longing for it that influences how we see the world and live our lives. Belonging is too often conditional upon fitting in, which causes us from a young age to hide what we fear will lead to rejection. Because this so often happens below our conscious radar, we are fragmented, concealing aspects of ourselves from ourselves. When we try to fit in from a place of conditional belonging, our lights are dimmed, and we lose access to that inner voice that is our most trusted advisor.

A revolution of the heart begins when we inhabit spaces where we can shed the masks we are wearing and undo what has been muted by conditional belonging. Although some of that work is internal, we can't ultimately do it alone. We need safe-enough spaces[2,3] where we can be authentic without encountering judgment or any other barrier to full participation. These places are vibrant communities, and in our culture there are too few of them, so we must create and nurture them ourselves.

Vibrant communities value the unique gifts that every member has to offer, and they rely upon everyone's input. Participating in these communities enables us to more clearly see the colossal cost exacted by the world of conditional acceptance, and it lets us dip our toes into another world that is possible.

A Choir That Uplifts All Voices

I first heard about the Harmony Project at the end of a conversation with Barbara Poppe, a consultant who works throughout the country with organizations and communities to help them find solutions to reduce homelessness and housing instability. We were speaking about her collaborative, community-oriented approach to addressing the complex problem of homelessness, though she acknowledged that for those impacted by poverty and homelessness, "it's hard to have community when there is extreme inequality going on."

Barbara uses a set of proven practices to design processes that engage everyone involved to find the best solutions for their circumstances. She believes a collaborative approach, where everyone's voice is included, is more effective than the typical top-down approach because "hierarchy does not build community and consensus."

She uses her leadership skills to surface the existing wisdom in the room, but she also makes sure the right people are present and that they are provided with the necessary data to lead to the best solutions. Barbara facilitates large meetings by bringing into the conversation a wide range of voices rather than a couple of dominant ones, so that all are engaged. One of her guiding principles is that everyone involved should bring more of themselves to the conversation than just the professional hat they wear.

She brought this style of leadership to the federal government when she worked in the Obama administration, serving as the executive director of the US Interagency Council on Homelessness. She recalled, "Bureaucrats were surprised that I really wanted to know what they thought. They were accustomed to getting approvals up the line. I became valued within the government because I got to a place where we really could do consensus building."

At the end of our conversation, I asked Barbara if she knew of a community that she thought I'd benefit from meeting. She lit up and told me about the Harmony Project, a community based in her home city.

"There is a movement that brings people together who want to sing, and they also do community service to help improve neighborhoods throughout Columbus, Ohio," she told me. "They put on huge concerts twice a year, and the people that go to them get inspired and want to be part of the movement. . . . You should consider going to one of their concerts."

⬤ ⬤ ⬤

What started as an interesting conversation led me to booking a flight to Columbus to attend the Harmony Project's summer concert and meet members of the choir. Thousands gathered at the Commons, an event space with a covered pavilion and a grand lawn. The crowd's atmosphere was palpably friendly; people sitting next to me asked if this was my first Harmony concert and warmly welcomed me.

The evening opened with a performance by the Columbus Children's Choir. Then the five-hundred-voice, nonauditioned community choir stepped out, joined by forty local musical artists and the Harmony Band and Orchestra.

Throughout the concert, choir members and other musical guests came forward for solo performances. When finished, they returned to their positions in the choir and received joyous hand slaps and high fives. I've never seen a choir who enjoyed themselves while performing like this one did. It was a celebration not only for the audience but also among themselves. As an audience member, I felt empathetic joy watching them support and encourage each other. For one night the choir and audience were joined together, part of a larger community.

Midway through the evening, twenty special guests stepped onto the stage: the Inside Out Choir, which is part of Harmony's programming with the residents in the Ohio Reformatory for Women, Ohio's largest women's prison. The women in the choir got permission to take leave to come and perform that evening. As they walked to the stage holding hands and wearing turquoise T-shirts, the crowd erupted in a show of support. They sang Lauren Daigle's "You Say," and there was hardly a dry eye in either the audience or the choir.

The lyrics of "You Say" speak to the doubt we sometimes feel about our worth and the lies we tell ourselves that we must overcome. It's a song about feeling as though we don't belong and moving beyond the past in order to claim our present. The words speak to the power of love, grace, and redemption. The lyrics not only resonated with the audience, but they also served in that moment to dissolve the barriers between us.

On the last note the audience erupted, jumping to their feet and cheering. Each member of the Inside Out Choir held up their hands in the shape of a heart, a familiar show of love and solidarity in Harmony choirs. As the women walked off the stage, the crowd continued to loudly show their appreciation.

There is magic in the remarkable diversity of a Harmony concert, including the range of musical talent within it. Beyond the uniqueness of the range of voices on display is the inspiration that comes from witnessing how they are equally celebrated. As David, the choir's director, says, "The strongest voices lift up the weakest ones." In the concert I attended, Kimberly Cocroft, a judge in the Franklin County Court, captivated the audience as she showed her impressive range while singing the Beatles' "Let It Be." She began singing at age three in the choir at Triedstone Missionary Baptist Church. Janine Dunmyre was next up to solo, singing a cover of Patti Smith's "People Have the Power." Janine had sung and played the piano in high school but as an adult had lost touch with her musical abilities. The Harmony Project helped her reclaim them. Now she enjoys traveling weekly as a Harmony volunteer to the Ohio Reformatory for Women, where she sings and talks with the women there.

The great variation in musical style and talent is matched by the diversity of backgrounds and lifestyles within the choir. People of different religions, races, economic circumstances, sexual orientations, and every other way we uniquely present in this world stand side by side in Harmony. The concerts are an extraordinary celebration of profound acceptance, true inclusion, and hospitality—qualities of vibrant community.

Even more than lifting up voices, Harmony's magic lies in its commitment to service, which draws choir members closer to each other. Everyone in the choir commits to contributing eight hours of service every six months. Choir members from forty of the county's sixty-four zip codes work next to each other, painting murals, planting trees, serving meals, building playgrounds, and transforming community centers.

When you add the total volunteer hours together, including hours logged by those who don't sing in the choir, the Harmony organization coordinates sixty thousand volunteer hours annually through more than four hundred volunteer projects. In terms of human effort, this investment in the city is worth more than $1.5 million. However, the value of so many hours of service offered from the heart is priceless.

What these numbers do not capture is the bonds that are forged between people when they volunteer together. The projects are intentionally coordinated to introduce choir members to other members whom they might not know. The Harmony organization also makes an effort to place people in an unfamiliar neighborhood when they do service projects. As volunteers work together, they can have conversations with each other that aren't possible during choir practice. It is here, working side by side, where they get to know each other as individuals, how they differ, and what they have in common.

● ● ●

Harmony Project was started in 2009 with a mission to build a strong, inclusive community through the vehicles of song and service. The idea behind it was that we can make an impact on healing the division that exists between us by bringing people together in the incubator of community and getting to know each other there.

David Brown founded Harmony in 2005 when, after sixteen years of leading choirs in major New York City churches, he found that the words *church* and *ministry* no longer rang true for him. He took a break from that work to explore questions such as, "Who am I? What is my place in the world?"

He visited friends in Columbus for quiet reflection and healing, and there the idea of combining music and service began to percolate. He envisioned hatching this project in LA, but his friends said, "Don't do it in LA. Try it in Columbus." His initial reaction was *No way*. David had enjoyed going to college in Columbus, but now he wanted to live somewhere more diverse and cosmopolitan. By coincidence, at that time he was offered and accepted a three-month position to promote local progressive candidates and the Obama 2008 campaign. In that window he began viewing Columbus in a different light and opened to the possibility of living there.

Columbus is like many other relatively affluent American cities in that it is diverse but racially segregated. The city has doubled in size in the past decade and continues its rapid growth. It is a progressive city, but the area surrounding it is conservative. Its residents are proud of their home, and they often describe Columbus as a big city with a small-town vibe.

David told me how his thinking around Columbus, and community, shifted:

I thought I could live here if my community looked like it did in LA or New York. If it was Jewish, Muslim, Christian, Buddhist, atheist, agnostic, LGBTQ, Black, Brown, white. In New York you have this all on one subway car. You don't have to work so hard for diversity. At the same time, you have to work harder there to build those deeper, meaningful relationships. In my experience with choir in New York, when the singing stopped, so did the harmony. Everyone went their own separate ways.

So I thought, "let's see if people would respond to the idea of using a choir as a not-so-subtle metaphor for a way to build community." The first months, I was aware of thinking "Columbus isn't this, or this." I began to realize that my lack of sense of community was because I was expecting people to be something they weren't. I realized I had started Harmony selfishly, because I wanted my community to be very diverse and to hold different opinions.

If I really want a diverse community, I now know it will be harder work than I thought. It means that if I am to be accepted for who I am, they don't have to be like me. It means I must accept myself for who I am and accept them for who they are. We have to figure out together how to live in community.

No one that participates in Harmony has to pay a dime to belong. They don't have to buy T-shirts. They don't even have to sell tickets. . . . You don't have to give, except service. For me, that's the true harmony we are trying to achieve—the social harmony, not musical harmony.

In service we intentionally put people together across zip codes and across other divides. When they get in those situations, our hope is that working together will promote natural conversations while planting trees, digging and sweating, or painting in a recreation center. And people will recognize that they like each other before they focus on their differences. What they have in common is, "We are here today because we believe that we both have something to give to this situation in this moment."

● ● ●

Reggie Jackson, Harmony Project's drummer, got hooked on the choir from his first rehearsal. "Before I started," Reggie said, "David told me that people didn't have to audition. I thought, 'Maybe this isn't the right gig for me.'" Reggie is a music teacher and an accomplished performer who has toured with jazz greats Diane Schuur and Dr. John, among others. "Then at that first rehearsal I was blown away by what David was able to do musically with people, some of whom had never sung before."

It was Harmony's diversity that pulled Reggie in and sealed his commitment. "We all have these subgroups we are part of, especially now in this country. And sometimes these provide us with a sense of safety. But they also separate us. It means a lot to me to have friends from the choir that are so different." Reggie shared how much he values having friendships with people from different racial, religious, political, and economic backgrounds who can work for community through the common thread of music.

"I admire how David has created an environment where those cliquish things that are in most communities don't exist," Reggie said. "I grew up playing in church my whole life. In the church community, I would be separated from the larger group because I was one of the musicians. And these subgroups, which are a barrier to connection, just don't happen in Harmony."

I asked Reggie how Harmony has successfully achieved diversity on so many levels, when many communities struggle to do the same. "It all comes down to acceptance," he replied. "The environment is about supporting each other in the courage to do something that you may not feel comfortable doing. This community has your back. Not only does it make you feel relaxed and at ease, but it is also encouraging and uplifting."

Reggie went on to talk about how he loves working with another choir affiliated with Harmony, made up of women and men with disabilities, because of their happiness and excitement when participating in the music. "Sometimes the music doesn't even matter as much as the joy they have in that moment. It reminds me of the joy I felt when I got my first drum set, that intense happiness. I see it in them at rehearsals."

At the time we spoke, racial tensions were running high between city residents and the police. As a Black man, Reggie was encouraged that city representatives were talking about race and racism in a way they hadn't before. I asked whether he believed a community like Harmony Project could add to the dialogue on race that was so needed. "Absolutely," he said. "How do we get there? We get there by having conversations where it's a safe environment, but also where I can ask to have them. It's so critical to have environments where we can have these conversations where people feel okay. If I'm not worried about offending, then I can take the risk to say what's on my mind and also learn from other people."

Song Is the Gateway to Community

From its beginnings in 2009 as an eighty-nine-person chorus, Harmony Project has become a choir of five hundred with a current waiting list of over seven hundred. In 2012, Harmony switched venues for its winter concerts and now performs them in the city's largest venue, the Nationwide Arena, which holds over eighteen thousand people.

Beyond the Harmony Community Choir, Harmony has numerous other musical and creative programs. In 2012, in collaboration with City Year Columbus, they initiated a weekly after-school arts and community service class to foster creativity, self-confidence, responsibility, and community engagement. Harmony's longest-running school program is based in South High School, in which nearly a third of the entire student body participates in an after-school chorus, South High Harmony. When the program began at South High, the students had low morale, and it was the lowest-performing school in its district. The students believed that people who didn't know them saw them as ignorant, ghetto, or out-of-line kids.[4]

As with the larger Harmony Community Choir, South High Harmony has no auditions, there is no cost to participate, and everyone commits to community service. The student choir performs in the biannual Harmony concerts on the largest stages in the city. Many of the kids in South High Harmony had never left Columbus; now, except for pandemic years, they take annual long-distance trips supported by Harmony to places like New York City and Washington, DC.

Students do have two additional requirements for participation that do not apply to the other choirs: good school attendance and grade improvement. (Harmony's partner, City Year Columbus, has services available to help students improve their academic performance.) There is also the expectation that choir members will be accepting and supportive of one another.

Harmony's community support of the South High students in the choir and the other extracurricular programs has been transformative. The impact of their efforts is reflected in both the teenagers' personal stories and in their graduation outcome results. Harmony's website shares the remarkable statistic that 100 percent of South High Harmony's seniors have successfully graduated.

• • •

Additionally, Harmony works with one hundred incarcerated women to create supportive community while they serve their sentences. (Melissa, whom we met in the introduction, shared how helpful this program had been to her.) Harmony also partners with other organizations to provide arts and recreation classes for men and women who have disabilities, who have experienced homelessness, or who have experienced mental health challenges, many of whom live below the poverty line. All in all, Harmony programs work with over one thousand people every single week.

Roni Burkes-Trowsdell was the warden of the Ohio Reformatory for Women when Harmony began its musical program there. She defies most depictions of prison wardens, eschewing a stance of power over others for a deep sense of responsibility toward the women she serves. Whether during her time as warden or in her current role overseeing nine state correctional facilities, she exudes warmth and respect in all her interactions. According to Melissa, "the [inmates] sense that she genuinely cares, and she feels free to show it when they care enough to work on themselves."

When David Brown came up with the idea to bring the Harmony community into the prison, he approached Roni to talk about his vision.

She shared her thoughts about their early meetings: "David is a burst of energy. All these ideas seem to come out of nowhere. He is so genuine in what he wants to do both in service and in wanting to connect people. His values I also hold strongly. So, I thought, 'David is either going to bring needed attention to this program, or he is going to get me fired. And I don't know which one it will be.'"

It was decided that the new choir would draw from the existing Tapestry program, where women lived together dormitory style rather than in separate cells.

Roni spoke more about her experience with Harmony and how the development of the choir within the prison unfolded:

David brought in people from the Harmony choir, and these people had no prior experience with corrections. They walked in with all kinds of feelings and judgments, which is normal. Then they saw people smiling at them and faces who looked like theirs. They saw women, some confident and some not. And they saw women who didn't want to be there but were trying to make the best of their time, trying to change their lives in positive ways.

That's where the true Harmony began. We very quickly started to see these internal walls that had divided us fall. These visitors became part of the Tapestry family.

I decided that if David and members of Harmony can come here and serve, then I can join the Harmony choir and serve there. I think David let me join the choir because I was the warden of the prison. Certainly not because of how I sing. People in Harmony care more about you as a person than how you sound. David wants us to sound good, don't get me wrong. But it's mostly about being a family.

What is beautiful and unique about Harmony is that assumptions aren't made about you. Members could care less what your title is. None of our differences matter when you walk through the doors of choir practice. Harmony has activities that make you communicate with the person near you. And during community service, we serve in ways that are often not in our initial comfort zone.

*When you look at the communities that Harmony serves,
they are so diverse, just like the choir. Diverse not only by race
but also how they are structured. From the prisons to the high
schools, we are asked to serve communities that are different
than those in which we live and work. And the person we serve
next to also comes from a different community. [During service
projects] the conversation often begins as something very basic:
"What's your name? Where are you from?" And then you move
to observations about the community you are serving. And then
maybe you talk about differences in life experiences.*

• • •

Vibrant communities create the experience of belonging that extends
beyond their membership. When other people are invited to participate
in different ways, the boundary between member and nonmember is
fuzzy, and participants have the experience of larger community. There
are many stories of how the Harmony Project has generated a spirit of
connection and service beyond its choirs.

Within the Ohio Reformatory for Women, the spirit of community
and service has blossomed beyond the Tapestry program. For example,
Cathe, a Harmony volunteer with the Tapestry program, introduced
the women to children living in Sunflower House, a hospice program
for children in South Africa with which she was also affiliated. Now
the women in Tapestry and the children in Sunflower House Skype
together every few weeks. The women sing to the children, and in turn,
the children sing back to the women. This is the power of community: a
loving and joyful connection is made across great distances and between
people who have felt the pain of marginalization.

The women of Tapestry have a desire to give back to others, and
they find ways to do so while serving their sentences. One year they participated in the Susan G. Komen Race for the Cure on prison grounds.
Sporting pink shirts, they were joined by staff in the walk for breast
cancer. In another example, the women made blankets for the family of
a police officer killed in the line of duty.

Roni Burkes-Trowsdell said that the experience of community spirit
and generosity has spread beyond the Tapestry program, which would

not have happened without the influence of Harmony. She spoke of the "lifers," women who will probably never leave prison, who one year raised over $100,000 to give to different organizations.

Vibrant community nourishes the innate desire to be of service that is within us all. It is inspiring to see how the spirit of generosity, nurtured by community, manifests in people who are living in extraordinarily challenging circumstances.

Creating Spaces Worthy of the Human Spirit

Physical spaces are the containers for communities. When we create such spaces intentionally, they promote connection, conversation, and pride of place. Community spaces that encourage connection and enjoyment should be everywhere, not only in those places that attract crowds or where people of economic privilege live. Let's prioritize the creation of these spaces in rural towns, suburbs, and cities, and especially when planning new developments. When we revitalize neighborhoods that have been neglected, with an eye toward making them more community-oriented, the psychology of the place changes. For example, when public art is installed in city neighborhoods, foot traffic and visibility increase, making them safer.[5] Creating beautiful spaces that promote community need not cost a lot of money.

Harmony's service projects are centered around revitalizing neighborhoods throughout Columbus. It's important that people from the neighborhoods who will be impacted by these projects meaningfully participate in them from the outset. When people join in the improvement of their own public spaces and then share them with others, it gives them a sense of belonging and pride in where they live. Harmony's members recognize this, and they know they need to join forces with individuals and organizations who have already been involved in caring for these neighborhoods. Harmony's partners on past projects have included local residents, grassroots organizations, small businesses, city council members, the recreation and parks department, and other nonprofits.

Harmony often focuses on one neighborhood per week, simultaneously working on projects big and small. One year the students from

South High Harmony picked up trash within one hundred blocks surrounding the area where they live and go to school. Helping their community gave them a sense of pride, and they felt empowered by making a difference. Nearby on Livingston Avenue, other choir members put a fresh coat of paint on a building that had seen better days. Some of these volunteers were living in Alvis House, a transition house for those recently released from prison to help them get a new start. And in Dreshler Park, volunteers planted trees, which will add beauty to the neighborhood while simultaneously offering shade and reducing pollution. Men from Alvis House and young children dug in the dirt together, singing songs while they planted trees.[6]

That same year, Harmony's biggest undertaking was creating a new playground, which required help from multiple businesses, dozens of organizations, and scores of volunteers. But before a shovel touched the ground, children from the neighborhood met in their local rec center and drew pictures of what they wanted their playground to look like. Their actual drawings were used in the designs for the park.[7]

Over seventy volunteers from both the local community and the organizations partnering with Harmony worked to prepare the lot for the eventual construction of the playground. On the day the playground was built, Kathy Spatz of Columbus Parks and Recreation said that over a hundred people came together in the cold rain to bring it to life. They included residents from the neighborhood and many others of all ages and from all zip codes within Columbus. One thing they had in common was that they were all happy to help create a park that the neighborhood's children would enjoy for years to come.[8]

One of Harmony's favorite service projects is creating murals throughout the city. The initial thought behind the mural project was to bring together as many people as possible and give them a shared artistic experience. Some of the volunteers painting the murals had some artistic training, whereas for others this was their first experience.

One year a mural spelling out the word *HOPE* was installed near Faith Mission, a homeless mission in downtown Columbus. Local artist Jeremy Jarvis, who designed the mural and coordinated the volunteers who painted it, sees the mural as a kind of architectural smile that he hopes will be a spark that helps get people through their day. Sue Villilo, who works at Faith Mission, saw that people who used the mission's services were gathering around the mural, talking to each other and taking selfies. She said she hoped the mural's message would lessen stereotypes about the homeless and people in poverty who work hard to change their situation.[9]

· · ·

When people collaborate to create vibrant communities, finding spaces to gather can be a real challenge. Cost of land and zoning restrictions are common obstacles for people trying to build community. Yet people are joining together, pooling their resources, and finding ways to creatively gather for the purpose of building authentic connection.

When I first met Jason Ikpatt, an artist and molecular biologist living in Austin, Texas, he had joined with a half dozen other people, all of whom were interested in exploring what it meant to live in community. Jason shared part of his motivation: "For those of us who feel that our opinions and feelings aren't valued in contemporary modern America, there's almost no place left to go."

When the group formed, they gathered in different places in Austin for conversations where they could explore what it meant to each of them to participate in a community. They experimented with what they called "focus weeks," in which they spent a week at a time working on different kinds of challenges individually and together. The purpose of the focus weeks was to help prepare them for living in a more community-oriented way.

For example, one week's challenge was to eat only food that they knew was grown, harvested, and sold fairly and ethically. The challenge was more difficult than they had imagined, and a few of them had very little to eat for a few days. By the end of the week, they had learned to forage locally, driving to farms and trading food with each other. Jason felt that the experience grounded them to themselves and each other, and they developed an appreciation of what it meant to labor together. The following week's focus was for each person to fulfill a need in their local geographical community, which required them to genuinely understand their neighbors' needs.

The cost of land in and around Austin is prohibitively expensive, so Jason and his community looked for land in other states that they could afford. One day he sent me an email with pictures of mountains and stunning topography, with his announcement that his community had purchased a thirty-eight-acre parcel in a flood plain in Portal, Arizona.

In preparation for spending time on the land, Jason created a movement practice that he calls a "bonding art," which he describes as a martial art, but loving. In this practice he incorporated dance elements he learned from his parents' traditions, who are Ibibio people from Nigeria. He also brought into the practice ways for two people to move in sync, mirroring each other's slow movements while maintaining eye contact. Jason told me he learned that moving in this slow, synchronized way has been shown to develop empathy and create deeper bonds between people. He calls this bonding practice *ukid iso,* which in the language of the Ibibio people means "seeing face."

It is as important to Jason's group to build community with the earth itself as it is to build community with each other. In addition to talking about geological permaculture, Jason and his community discuss social permaculture. For example, how do they create an environment that will allow both water and people to easily flow in ways that enrich the environment?

The group travels to Portal, Arizona, at least twice a year and is developing plans for staying on the land for longer periods of time. Every few months Jason and I catch up on Zoom, and our conversations center around questions and insights about community. After our friendship developed online, in 2022 I traveled to Austin, Texas, to meet him in person along with his other community members. I look forward to the day I meet them in Portal to see in person what they have built, relationally and concretely, in harmony with the land.

The Shift from In Person to Online

Online communities are here to stay, and they make it possible for people to connect in ways that were not possible before. The phrase "online communities" means many different things and represents many kinds of ways of interacting with each other. Because of this, studies show conflicting results of both the benefits and the potential harm of these communities to our psychological health and collective well-being. We have barely begun to understand the implications of a major shift in how we interact socially, spending less time in person and more online.

When we engage online communities intentionally, they are an invaluable complement and enhancement to our in-person communities and are vitally important in and of themselves. They are also potential sources of relationships that can later become in-person ones. Over half of teenagers say they have made new in-person friendships that began online.[10]

When meeting in person is not possible, meeting online enhances a sense of connection. For those from groups whose stories are underrepresented, such as people with disabilities, online communities are a place to share their experiences, providing validation and support that is often missing in a culture of ableism. Elderly people who are less mobile can stay connected to lifelong friends whose stories they share, people who see them for who they are, as being so much more than someone who is aging and in ways more vulnerable. Most of us have valued relationships that have been sustained or enhanced across distances because of readily available online access.

Online communities provide the opportunity to have meaningful interactions with people in different parts of the country or world and with dramatically different life experiences, expanding our minds while reminding us of our common humanity. Earlier in the book, a wonderful example of this was how women in prison in the US Midwest built heartfelt connections with children in South Africa. And communities in the trenches of environmental or social-justice work, which places them at high risk for burnout, can be energized by online communities where they meet other people doing similarly important work.

The online communities that most cultivate qualities of vibrant community are those that offer the opportunity to have face-to-face and authentic interactions with others. Yet face-to-face interactions online don't give us the same access to nonverbal cues, which might be necessary to foster high-quality social interactions. Conversations can unfold more organically and naturally in person, shifting between people more effortlessly, than on camera. And, of course, physical touch, a powerful way of showing care and empathy, is only available to us in person. Still, we are adaptive social creatures and can share who we are, care for each other, and let ourselves be vulnerable within online communities.

• • •

We also need to acknowledge the ways in which online communities are a major time suck and don't challenge us to relate to each other in healthy ways. The sheer number of hours collectively spent online interferes with gathering in person and showing up for one another. For example, studies suggest that limiting time spent on social media to thirty minutes a day is good for our mental health.[11] And yet, in 2020 Americans spent on average three hours a day on social media,[12] 600 percent more than is recommended for healthy connection. The same study found that the average American spends nearly an hour a day on Facebook alone. As a clinician, I've seen how a frequent source of conflict between parents and children centers around the time spent on devices and the sites being visited.

It should be of deep concern to everyone that social media corporations have put tremendous effort into making their platforms habit-forming and even addictive. Child advocacy groups are trying to find ways to hold companies that intentionally design apps with addictive features accountable for the social and emotional costs to children.[13]

• • •

We can engage in healthy ways with our online communities by reflecting on questions such as these: Is this a space that promotes interacting with each other in ways that show care? Is there a general atmosphere of acceptance, and do people feel free to voice a range of viewpoints? Are skillful ways for handling tensions and conflict offered in the form of guidelines, and does the community respect them? Does the community celebrate each other and find effective ways to create meaning together? Does the community find ways to welcome authentic member input, and is it a platform that encourages people to be hospitable toward each other? Am I practicing skills that are conducive to vibrant community when I participate in my online communities? And in those communities where I am not able to do so, can I decrease the amount of time spent in them? The more we can answer these questions in the affirmative, the more likely it is that our time spent online can enhance our relationships and sense of healthy belonging.

Everyone Can Be a Leader

Vibrant communities have more dynamic, relational models of leadership than those seen in top-down communities, where leadership is in the hands of a few people. A community-based form of leadership uses practices such as active listening and positive, skillful inquiry, without being highly structured. As Barbara Poppe discussed earlier in this chapter, a community-focused model engages all members' participation, and everyone takes responsibility for showing leadership at different times and in different ways.

With more inclusive leadership, individuals are better able to bring their strengths and skills to the group and the task at hand. For example, when Barbara trained her staff in the Obama administration in practices that encourage leadership within the entire group, she quickly noticed a shift in how they planned and interacted among themselves and with stakeholders. Unlike typical large meetings where only a few people speak, this kind of training led to a much wider range of voices participating in the conversation.

Barbara, who had been part of an intentional community when she was younger, shared that an inclusive style of leadership is her natural way of relating, but she lost her way for a time when she became an executive. When she later trained in community leadership principles, she found herself again in alignment with her core beliefs and now cannot imagine working any other way.

Barbara believes that the practices of community-based leadership must be used wisely in order to generate good decisions and helpful outcomes. She disagrees with a frequent assumption of these models that all the wisdom that is needed is already in the room, and it just needs to be unlocked. Barbara has seen how these helpful process tools can still lead to unhelpful solutions "when you don't have the right people in the room and [then the group] makes decisions, for example, out of their middle-class, white, privileged background."

It takes leadership skills to facilitate the process by which communities find their own best solutions. Parker Palmer, an author who has written for decades about community and leadership, observes that "leadership in a bureaucracy is a piece of cake compared to leadership for community. Leadership for a community is more like conducting an orchestra, or like good teaching, where you turn people loose on something. Rather than just fall into chaos, you set ground rules and practices for what unfolds." Further discussion of these ground rules or principles will be presented in chapter 5.

Traditional Indigenous ways of leadership are a good example of how to support vibrant community, and many community-based forms of leadership are modeled after them. Vince Two Eagles and Amy Doom, who cofacilitated dialogue circles focused on racism in South Dakota and whose work will be discussed in chapter 5, offer their thoughts on community-oriented dialogue.

Vince says, "The word *chief* is not in Native vocabulary. *Spokesperson* is a more accurate way to describe leadership. The collective periodically selects someone who has the best skills for whatever faces the community at the time. The same goes with the structured leadership that was used in the dialogues on racism that Amy and I participated in. It doesn't try to impose ideas of how communities ought to develop. Instead, it uses the dialogue process to facilitate solutions that come out of group discussions."

Amy adds, "In Native culture, the groups make the decisions in a circle. In dominant culture we are authoritative—the leader makes decisions for all because they were elected or chosen in some way. But in Native circles the person who has been called into the circle is called upon to do a very specific task. They go back to the circle when the task is over because their leadership is bestowed only when there is group consensus for them to be there."

● ● ●

Parker's metaphor for community-based leadership as resembling conducting an orchestra is an apt one in reference to the Harmony Project. As the founder and creative director of the Harmony choirs, David Brown is the leader during choir rehearsals and on the stages where the choirs perform. He is also a general force of nature within the organization. His humor and energy are infectious, and everyone I spoke to from Harmony smiles when his name comes up. At the same time, David's presence does not overshadow the collaborative spirit as reflected in the stories people shared with me about their personal experiences in Harmony. In this vibrant community there is room for it all, and for everyone.

In all my conversations, people shared personal stories of how their experience of Harmony was about more than the choir and the performances. They offered examples of how they reached beyond their personal comfort levels to show initiative in Harmony programs, and they also shared how other members had done the same in ways that had made a positive impact on them.

Within the Harmony program housed in the Ohio Reformatory for Women, there are wonderful examples of community leadership shown by the prison administration, the Harmony volunteers, and the women who are incarcerated. Roni Burkes-Trowsdell partnered with David in the Harmony vision by making the choir possible there. In her role as warden, she supported the program in which inmates sing to terminally ill children in South Africa, and she encouraged the women's initiatives to support other communities outside the prison.

Another example is how Susie, a choir member and volunteer with the Inside Out Choir, initiated and led a writing group within the Tapestry program. Melissa participated in this writing group while she was in Tapestry, and she credits the group—both for its writing exercises and for the emotional support it provided—with helping her heal from trauma and own her life moving forward. Melissa believes that the fact that Susie is a professional executive who led the group in a caring, collaborative way enabled her to see herself in a new light. Susie showed care for Melissa outside of the writing group and would FaceTime her daily after she was released, reminding Melissa of everything she had to be proud of.

   Vibrant communities foster environments where everyone takes initiative with the goal of benefiting the entire community and beyond. That this is possible even in a restrictive environment like a prison is a testament to what is possible when we cultivate communities where everyone is valued and is invited to lend their voices and offer up their gifts.

chapter 2

a common commitment to care

*The really important kind of freedom involves
attention . . . and being able truly to care about
other people and to sacrifice for them, over and
over, in myriad petty little unsexy ways, every day.[1]*
　　　　　　　　　　　　　　　— DAVID FOSTER WALLACE

We experience belonging within our communities when we practice
caring for each other, both in giving and in receiving it. Virtually anything we say or do can be a gesture of care if offered in the spirit of care.
Care manifests in a kind word, the willingness to listen, a gesture, an
affirming touch, a pause, and the recognition of someone's gifts. It is,
among other things, consideration, kindness, respect, effort, compassion, understanding, patience, and sharing.

Fostering empathic relationships should begin early in life, and we
help children by demonstrating for them that we care about caring.
Children who show caring behaviors at a young age, such as by sharing
and cooperating with others, exhibit other strengths in school as they
get older. For example, children who are more helpful to other children
in first grade have higher reading skills in third grade.[2] Although some
children more spontaneously show caring behavior, all can learn to do
so when these behaviors are modeled for them. Children as young as
eighteen months mirror altruistic behavior.[3]

Research in other settings shows that when we show care in how we
communicate with each other, we feel better. When health care provid-
ers explicitly show care for patients by communicating in a collaborative
way, patients recover faster and have better mental health outcomes following an illness.[4] Nurses who can take time to be more caring toward
their patients are happier on the job.[5] Clearly, fostering an environment
that prioritizes the expression of care between people is the best medicine. And a body of research shows that nurturing work environments
characterized by interest, support, and respect greatly benefit employees, employers, clients, and the bottom line.[6]

When our communities value expressions of care between people,
we experience belonging, and by extension we are healthier, happier,
and more engaged.

Getting to the Heart of Home

Just a couple miles outside the city limits of Austin, Texas, lies a community of inclusion like no other. Community First! Village sits on a fifty-one-acre parcel of land and has more than five hundred homes for men and women who had been chronically homeless, most of whom are over fifty years old. The village housing, built in two phases, consists of 330 two-hundred-square-foot tiny homes designed by architects from the world over, along with over two hundred RVs.

Far more than a collection of tiny homes and RVs, the village was designed to nurture the spirit of caring and belonging. Alan Graham, its founder, explains: "People here have a new chapter. It's not about fixing or repairing anyone. These people are the most vulnerable and, until now, have been outcasts. It's essential they have permanent housing, security, and a caring community."

The layout of the village intentionally maximizes the opportunity for neighbors to spontaneously interact with each other. There are front doors and porches but no backyards or back doors, and plenty of outdoor spaces where people can gather. Because sharing meals is an important way to build community, in addition to well-equipped outdoor kitchens there are also barbecue pits, a community table, and other places for people to eat together.

The first resident moved into the community in 2016. When I visited just two years later it already looked like a well-established village. The postage stamp–size yards are well maintained and have personal touches. The public spaces are lively, yet the homes, in near proximity, still offer privacy to residents. Although visitors are welcome in all the public spaces, their presence doesn't interfere with the daily lives of those living there.

On that first visit, I saw an Art House, a modern blacksmith shop, a community garden and labyrinth, and a volunteer-run Community Store where villagers and visitors congregate. There is also the Community Cinema, a five-hundred-seat amphitheater that is a favorite venue for Austinites to come enjoy a movie. While watching the movie, guests enjoy snacks from the Community Grille, an on-site food truck. The cinema is a gift from Austin's iconic Alamo Drafthouse, which partners with Community First! Village to present a free Friday Movie Night.

Next to the movie theater is the Community Inn, one of the country's largest tiny-home B and Bs. Visitors to Austin can choose to stay in a tiny home, a trendy Airstream trailer, or a teepee. They can buy food provisions and art and crafts made by villagers at the Community Store. There is also an on-site auto shop that offers car washes, detailing, and oil changes, performed by technicians in the village who were trained by a local Toyota dealership. And there is an event venue that can be rented for weddings, musical or dance performances, conferences, or film premieres, with the option of on-site catering.

Everyone who lives in the village pays rent ranging from $250 to $500 a month. Most of the residents qualify for disability, a system out of touch with the cost of living anywhere in this country. Residents have ample opportunity for dignified work within the village so they can meet their rent requirements and cover other basic needs.

● ● ●

On my second visit, I stayed for a few nights at the Community Inn in a state-of-the-art Airstream. The weather was unseasonably cold and rainy the entire time. Because of this, people were inside their homes, and the village was uncharacteristically quiet. When I wandered into the Art House, I encountered only one person, Ute Dittemer, who can be found there making art on every day it is open.

Ute has a distinguished look, with close-cropped white hair and striking ice-blue eyes. She has a wonderful sense of humor that, when it quietly surfaced, initially seemed in contrast with her serious presence. When we first met, she asked me what I was looking for, and I felt like an interloper disturbing her at work. But when I expressed interest in her paintings, Ute graciously stopped what she was doing and showed me more of them as well as some of her clay sculptures.

I immediately recognized Ute's sculptures because a friend who had joined me on my first trip to the village had purchased one of her pieces. It was a sugar bowl in the shape of a mythical horse that now holds pride of place on her dining room table. Many of Ute's sculptures can be described as a marriage of realism and whimsy. In her humanlike figures, which to me resemble magical beings, Ute tries to convey a sense of serenity and expanded consciousness.

Ute first started drawing as a child in Germany; shapes and colors have always taken her on a journey in which the outside world fades. Before coming to live in the village she had never worked with clay. She immediately took to the medium and described it like a meditative practice: "When I work with clay, it is soft and fragile, allowing me to move it in any direction. But you have to be careful; [when you] touch it very lightly it changes. Like a child, it is malleable but often goes off in its own direction. As I let go of my expectations of the end result, something more beautiful often appears. Sometimes I am stunned, looking at what has been created."

In 2019, Ute's clay sculptures were prominently displayed at the yearly Village of Lights, a four-day village event where over two hundred thousand lights are choreographed to holiday music. The festival features a holiday arts-and-crafts fair, as well as an auction, with all proceeds going directly to the residents who are the makers. Ute's thirty-two-piece hand-carved chess set was featured in the festival's auction. The set took her six months to complete and included an accompanying booklet that told the story of each chess piece. The starting bid for her exquisite creation was $10,000.

● ● ●

Ute and I so enjoyed our interaction that we agreed to meet again the following evening to continue the conversation. When we did, she shared more of her life leading up to coming to live in the village. Ute grew up in Germany and loves animals. One of her earliest memories is of her father buying her and her sister a donkey. She worked in a steady government job for fourteen years, loves to travel, and has a sense of adventure. When she was younger, she was in an abusive relationship that was hard to leave because she had two young sons. Ute's unhealthy habit is smoking cigarettes, and she has had periods of severe depression. Many people would find aspects of Ute's personal story relatable, except for the fact that she was homeless for nearly ten years. Because of this, Ute has experienced profound marginalization.

Once someone is homeless, the isolation that results from losing possessions and connections to family and friends can be devastating. And the stigma of homelessness makes it difficult for those experiencing it to reach out for help. Ute lost touch with family when she was homeless, but now she is in frequent contact with her sister and sons.

Ute is grateful that she can now enjoy the solitude necessary for her creative life. "I very much value having time to myself because I didn't have any on the streets [where] you're always out in the open and sur-rounded by people. Maybe you can be alone in a bathroom if you get lucky," she added with a laugh.

Ute lived with her husband, Mike, and their cat, Maui, in a village RV until they recently moved into a micro home in the newest section of the village's development. The couple first met in 2005 at Barton Springs, a natural hot-spring pool warm enough for year-round swimming, which is a favorite public gathering place in Austin. Mike was working at a bar at the time but lost his job—"it's harder to find work the older you get," he told me—and they became homeless in 2008.

Before they met, Mike had his own painting company. But he lost everything when he was literally struck by lightning and went into a coma for two months. When he was released from the hospital, his trucks and equipment were gone. He still had visible burns on his face and arms. According to Mike, "I was [physically] okay but I still had emotional issues. I had red skin [which] damaged my positive energy for years. I tried and tried until I just kind of gave up. Eventually I got evicted."

Ute and Mike sometimes dream of living in a neighborhood where not everyone has a common history of homelessness, though they love their home in the village. Ute said, "I feel calm knowing that I have a home. I have the basics like a shower, dishes that I can wash, and a stove I can cook on."

Mike added, "I have a home where I don't get bit up by mosquitoes or have police tell me in the middle of the night that I have to move. And Ute has a chance to earn decent money making art for people who love her work."

There is a bank of windows in my home that I frequently gaze out of, and on a side table nearby sits Azlyn, a treasured Ute sculpture. Azlyn is a lion that is both gentle and fierce, its name a Turkish derivative of the lion Aslan from *The Chronicles of Narnia*. Ute and I stay in touch, and I am fortunate to call her my friend.

• • •

Community First! Village is Alan Graham's dream and brainchild. Twenty-plus years ago, he was working in real estate and raising a family when he felt called to live in service to the homeless. What began as one food truck delivering meals to men and women without shelter developed into an entire fleet of vehicles and the nonprofit Mobile Loaves and Fishes. To date, twenty thousand volunteers have served over five million meals to people living on the streets of Austin.

"As I developed relationships with these men and women on the street, I saw how awesome they were," said Alan. "I wanted to spend real time in relationship with them. They are the most honest people in that they share their vulnerability, whereas you and I are taught to mask whatever defects we have."

Alan began to organize street retreats where people had the direct experience of sleeping on the streets for two to three days and nights. From the beginning, men and women who were homeless were protective of Alan and those he brought on these retreats. They guided the retreatants to relatively safe areas and gave them tips for how to survive while homeless. In the fifteen or so years between the first retreat and when I last spoke to Alan, he has personally spent over two hundred nights on Austin's streets.

When you talk to Alan, it is immediately evident that he is a straight shooter who loves to connect with people. "Spending time with my homeless friends, being willing to talk to people who may smell of urine or multiday body odor, I went beyond my mind's boundary that limited me and began to mine the gold nuggets of their awesomeness," he said. "Their transparent vulnerability helped me come face to face with a personal choice: whether I would continue with my own veil. I came from a dysfunctional family. Was I willing to share that I've snorted cocaine or that I got arrested at fourteen for stealing a car? . . . We are dying to share with people who can relate and will not condemn us."

Alan's dream went beyond feeding those who were homeless; he wanted to find ways to give them homes. When he and his family went on summer vacations, they'd often stay in RV parks. He noticed that there was an inherent sense of community in those parks; someone could pull in with a million-dollar Prevost motorhome and park it right next to a used Jayco Bunkhouse trailer. So, the first step toward his bigger dream was purchasing a $5,000 RV and placing it in a privately owned RV park. "And fourteen years later I am sitting in the middle of an RV park on steroids . . . that, to me, is the greatest place to live on the planet."

● ● ●

It took Alan years to convince potential neighbors that a village of the most vulnerable was a good idea. His first attempt to build a community for the chronically homeless took place on land located inside Austin's city limits. He described the process as brutal: "We were yelled at, spit on, the police were called. It was amazing."

He looks back at that failure as a blessing because of what came next: purchasing fifty-one acres just outside Austin's municipal boundaries, where the zoning is much more flexible. Through his enthusiasm and entrepreneurial skills, Alan attracted a huge amount of financial support from individuals, organizations, and businesses. This funded the entire first phase of the village of 130 tiny homes and one hundred RVs, along with public spaces. Then local government lent support, building sidewalks, providing electrical and sewer access, and adding a bus stop people can use to get from the village to downtown Austin.

Once they broke ground for the village's first phase, everything happened with remarkable speed. Droves of volunteers showed up, and it wasn't long before residents were able to move into their new homes.

Within the first year of people moving in, an attitude of "not in my backyard" gave way to open-hearted participation. Not only was the community accepted by its neighbors; many people asked to join in and be part of it. For example, Alan was walking the fence line one day when a young woman with a toddler approached him from the other side. She told him she owned the adjacent land and asked him if he would mind if she built a gate abutting his property so she could have direct access to the community. Alan responded, "You're damn right you can! I'll pay for it!"

Alan believes that every one of us longs for more of what is offered in the village: caring community. "When we get out of the comfort zones that limit us and show care by meeting face to face with people who live literally next door or down the street, then we can begin to move the needle," he said. "When we welcome people into community, regardless of whether they have a house or [not], then we understand profoundly what it means to be home."

For Alan, this is just the beginning of a movement that he believes is a blueprint for successfully addressing the country's homelessness problem. But there are still a tremendous number of human beings who live on the streets of Austin. In January 2021, the Ending Community Homelessness Coalition estimated that there were 3,160 homeless people in Austin and Travis County, of which over 2,200 were unsheltered and living in places not fit for human habitation.[7] In this same counting, they also estimated that 51 percent of the total number of people without a place to live are chronically homeless.

Mobile Loaves and Fishes continues to serve meals daily, and some village residents now volunteer their time to help feed their brothers and sisters still out on the streets. The organization has assisted in the launch of food truck programs in other cities, including Minneapolis, Nashville, and New Orleans.

In April 2021 it was announced that Community First! Village had plans for a large expansion of the microhome development in 2022. The organization purchased 127 additional adjacent and nearby acres through a gift from the Tito's vodka company philanthropy program. The expansion began in 2022 and will occur in two phases, which will add 1,400 more microhomes and additional community facilities when complete. When all phases of the village are complete, a significant portion of those in Austin who are chronically homeless will have a permanent home to call their own and a community that cares about them.

"People who have experienced what is happening here, who have opened their minds and hearts, no longer see the homeless problem as intractable," Alan said. "What we do is provide a sense of home and transform the way that people view the homeless."

Imperfect and Beautiful Community

There is no vibrant community of authentic human beings without vulnerability. Some communities include people whose vulnerabilities make it difficult for them to take on the same responsibilities as other members. Communities of the future are ones that can make room for people who need a greater degree of support. One like Community First! Village, whose members have been overwhelmingly marginalized and have nearly all experienced significant trauma, presents unique challenges.

One of the foundations of vibrant community is the capacity to build trusting relationships. Many people who have been on the streets have had a collapse of their social support system, or they never had one in the first place, which can make it difficult for them to enter into trusting relationships. Richard Devore, who runs and harvests the community garden in the village, describes himself as a lifelong loner.[8] Since childhood he never felt he fit in and was not comfortable around people. "That probably made them uncomfortable around me," he observed.

The social and emotional problems that some people experienced before homelessness and that can result from living on the streets don't just go away. There are deep wounds left from major trauma that may never fully heal. Ute said, "We are encouraged to care for each other, but it can be difficult. Many people have mental health challenges [and] it's not like in most other neighborhoods where you have the same challenges, but they are more spread out among a greater number of people."

A vibrant community of vulnerable human beings requires a protective envelope that provides a sense of adequate safety. Everyone is a valued member of community, but for some it takes time to heal and learn healthy ways of coping and relating to each other. Within the village there are mental health services on site for residents, including psychotherapy and a program to treat substance abuse. As essential as social services are, an even more beneficial resource is the community's pervasive caring atmosphere.

Richard, who was homeless on and off for thirteen years, had resigned himself to being a drug addict on the streets. For him the most impactful thing about moving into Community First! Village was having a place of his own to relax without being told to pick up his things and move. After two years of living there, he is now very active with different groups within the village. As someone who used to feel he never belonged, he now leads tours of the garden and the village. Richard's perceptions of himself have transformed, from a loner to someone who values and is capable of deep connection. And he shows care outside his community by volunteering on the food trucks, serving up meals for those who aren't as fortunate as he now is.

There are high rates of mental illness among the homeless, but there are also high and rising rates among the entire population within the United States. Lack of a supportive community and of access to mental health care is often more destructive to a person's stability than the illness itself. Some people are homeless as a result of severe chronic mental illness, such as schizophrenia or bipolar disorder. But when you hear people's stories in the village, you understand that most often a crisis, such as the loss of a job, or a tragedy, such as the death of a child, is more likely the start of a person's downward trajectory.

Many villagers have histories of alcohol and drug addictions, illnesses that often require multiple attempts at treatment, and some still use substances. Alan said addiction in the village is not as pervasive as stereotypes would suggest. "When you live in a place this size, we know each other's business, because we care," he said. As long as addictive behaviors don't negatively impact the community, they are tolerated. If a resident stops paying rent or is disruptive to the community because of their drug or alcohol use, they are asked to leave.

But, in general, people are given leeway to live their lives as they wish because they are autonomous adults. Sometimes people have loud arguments that need to be broken up. What is never tolerated is crime, which is not generally a problem in the village. Although people are occasionally asked to leave, there is an extraordinary 85 percent retention rate.

Most residents qualify for disability, yet this designation says nothing of their contributions to the community, because they are what makes the village vibrant. This is why we must focus on community as the primary container for a healthy society, because everyone has abilities that benefit the collective.

Caring Is a Two-Way Street

An important part of the village's safety envelope is provided by volunteers who make up nearly 20 percent of the population. From a variety of professional backgrounds such as health care, teaching, and finance, the volunteers offer their professional skills to the community. Because the volunteers and the other villagers have very different life experiences, there can be a two-tiered social stratification between them.

Ute described this divide that she sometimes experiences as "an invisible border" in which volunteer community members interact with each other differently than they do with villagers who had experienced homelessness. Ute explained: "[The volunteers'] interactions can stay on a level of giver/receiver. Sometimes I wish I lived where nobody knows that you were homeless before. Because when they discover this . . . people can close up and not share equally anymore."

My friendship with Ute has given me the opportunity to watch my own internal thoughts that "otherize" people. She helped me become more conscious of thought bubbles along the lines of "my friend Ute who was once homeless." I am grateful to her for helping me shine a light on ways of thinking that keep me separate from others.

Imagine if you were defined by others, for all time, by painful life circumstances or by only one aspect of who you are. How would it feel if people think about you as the person who was out of work for a year, or has an anxiety disorder, or had difficulty leaving an abusive relationship?

It would feel demoralizing to have others view our vulnerabilities and difficulties as a way of defining us into the future. And yet this is exactly how our culture conditions us. What is acceptable or what is the norm is not labeled, and what lies outside that is named as *other*.

Even if we don't intend to make anyone feel separate and don't verbalize differences, the effects of othering are still felt. And this habit of mind causes us to hide away aspects of ourselves that would be viewed as other, keeping us from being fully authentic.

When people who have been marginalized and have struggled mightily to accept themselves in an inhospitable world find a community where they can be themselves, they often wear fewer masks than those who have been accepted into the mainstream.

Although there is social stratification within the village, there is also a unique opportunity through relationship building to challenge notions of difference and lessen the impact of oppressive labels we assign to ourselves and others.

Most programs of service to the homeless are unidirectional, with one group doing for the other. Although these may provide an important function, such as feeding people or providing shelter, they are not transformative. The kind of caring that transforms us is always bidirectional; we both give care and receive it. For those living in the village who have never been homeless, there is the opportunity to challenge stereotypes they may still have. Likewise, those who have experienced soul-crushing marginalization now have the healing opportunities that come from making valued contributions within their communities.

Personal Stories Lead to Understanding

A commitment to care means that we seek to understand before we judge, and the path to understanding is through listening to each other's personal stories. It's easier to care for someone when we can relate to them, and our perspectives and beliefs align. Caring that really stretches us and opens the door to deeper connection often starts when we don't understand one another, but we sincerely wish and intend to get there.

People who are different from us in ways that make us uncomfortable provide excellent opportunities to practice understanding. It is in these relationships that we can notice all the ways our minds judge. It's not as if our minds will completely stop judging, because that's what minds do sometimes. But we can better notice and take responsibility for our judgments, seeing them as more about ourselves, which can transform our relationship to them.

Understanding is an active process that takes time, a willingness to come to the conversation and give the other person our attention. It sometimes means breathing into our constrictions when we feel uncomfortable or when we bristle at what someone is telling us. Breathing and pausing enable us to slow down so we don't quickly place what we are hearing into our mind's preexisting boxes.

• • •

Although Alan is passionate about his faith and personal beliefs, he embodies acceptance of the paths of others. "What we are creating is a banquet table of inclusion," he explained. "And at the table of inclusion, which everyone desires, who do we exclude?" For Alan, the answer is "no one," and his inclusion is unconditional.

Alan had a close friendship with Laura, a transgender woman he met on his first street retreat years earlier. Before their friendship deepened, he had a lack of understanding and appreciation for gender identities other than his own cisgender one. One of Alan's favorite memories from their friendship happened on a day he got injured while he was working on a food truck. As he was lying on the ground in pain, Laura picked him up with strong, gentle hands and cared for him.

This experience was transformative because in that moment, Alan understood that he could love and fully accept someone without needing to understand their life choices. He credits Laura as being key to his acceptance of people from different walks of life and with different lifestyles. "She taught me a unity beyond diversity, a beauty of acceptance beyond understanding," he said.

Born to an English father and Navajo mother, at twelve Laura left her home on a New Mexico reservation and got on a bus to Austin with hopes of working in technology. Laura endured complex trauma that led to severe depression, job loss, and a continued cycle of homelessness. She persisted and got a GED, a bachelor's degree, and a master's degree in electrical engineering, mostly while living on Austin's streets with an old laptop and a single change of clothes.

Laura would have been one of the first people to move into a home in Community First! Village upon its completion but was hit by a car that ran a red light in a busy intersection. She developed an infection from her injuries that proved fatal. Because hospital visiting privileges did not extend to close friends and chosen family, Laura could not have the people she touched and loved at her side as she died.

Alan describes Laura as an unlikely hero in the life that she led. She knew best how to care for and serve people, not with a checkbook but with an enormous, open heart. While living on the fringe and receiving virtually no compassion herself as a transgender woman on the streets, she found ways to care for others without judgments or boundaries. "She couldn't give money, but she dedicated her life to caring for others," said Alan. "She organized clothing donations for women and tutored in math and science. The amount she gave was extraordinary because of the love she gave."

• • •

On my first visit to the village, I was invited to participate in a welcome ceremony that was happening for a new member who was moving in that day. People from the village and guests brought food in a moving display of hospitality, and the new villager said a few words. Someone had made him a quilt for his new home. He knew people in the village whom he had met from the Mobile Loaves and Fishes food trucks, and they were there to welcome him. Because I was a stranger and guest myself, it was a gift to be invited to participate in this ritual where I could welcome this man to his new home, and he in turn reached out and offered me a warm hug. Leaving that day, I imagined how we would relate to each other differently if everyone was welcomed in this way—to their new apartments, or homes, or places of employment—with a short ceremony and the sincere message that they are an important addition.

The welcome celebration was Christian-forward in its language; for example, it included Bible passages as part of the welcome. Yet in the village, where the spiritual offerings are Christian in flavor, there is no pressure to participate in any faith community; all beliefs are respected and welcome.

Still, I couldn't help but think of the conundrum that although community rituals are necessarily culturally specific in their language, it is tricky when the culture has a millennia-long history of trying to convert people to their way of thinking. It's an important question to think about: in our communities, how can we honor the traditions that deepen our bonds, while also grappling with the ways in which these same traditions have impeded care when they have not honored or included people on different paths?

The beauty of vibrant communities is their ability to continually reinvent themselves, discovering new, more evolved ways of practicing care.

● ● ●

Ute introduced me to Haley, a young woman who moved to the village in 2018. She may be the youngest person in the village who had been homeless. Haley has a somewhat different experience from other villagers in that she wasn't living on the streets, but she could not lift herself up from an in-and-out cycle of homelessness. She stayed at the Salvation Army shelter for nine months in order to qualify to live in Community First! Village. Haley knew the village well because she would frequently visit her father, an artist who was one of the first residents there.

Haley credits the volunteers with being important role models, showing her how to meaningfully participate in community. When she first moved there, "everyone knew my name and said 'hi' a hundred times a day. It was kind of weird, but I valued being noticed everywhere I went."

Describing herself as shy, she said that in the past she felt sad and angry much of the time. Feeling this way made it hard for her to become involved with other people.

Now Haley works at the Community Inn. One day in a work meeting she heard the inn's manager, Taylor, say, "Our goal is to have everyone out here involved in service to others in this community." Haley had never heard this said before and it made her want to try it. She gave an example of showing up for someone's birthday party, something that in the past she would have avoided because of social anxiety. Haley now views showing up for others as a form of service and it has become less uncomfortable. "I'm no longer nervous that I'm going to screw up and do something stupid," she said.

Haley has suffered profound loss in her life, including "the mega trauma of losing your kids," and says her internal voice still often knocks her down. But with the encouragement of people in the village, she is starting to learn how to build herself up, and she sometimes catches herself when she puts herself down. There are even moments when she tells herself what is right about her.

Experiencing care every day from people within the community builds Haley up little by little. The deep pain that she still feels is sometimes unbearable and may never go away. She relates to the need to sometimes numb herself from such intense pain. But she also feels happiness living in the village. And she is hopeful for a future where she can again have a relationship with her children.

Now Haley finds purpose in helping others. "I'm helpful anywhere I can, anytime I can. I'm literally looking for the next person to help."

● ● ●

I've noticed that people from some faith-based traditions are skilled at showing up for community. It aligns with their values, and from my perspective, this is one of the most beautiful aspects of these traditions. Nearly everyone I spoke with for this book who has an affiliation with a particular faith tradition had a perspective that it is community, and not an institution, that is at the heart of the tradition. This definition of faith is like Martin Luther King Jr.'s version of "beloved community," which is a community of justice where everyone is cared for and there is no hunger, poverty, or hate.

To experience true belonging, we need to have our personal stories reflected in our communities. And, certainly, our beliefs and faith traditions are an important part of our personal stories. The challenge for vibrant communities that value true inclusion is for their members to honor and observe their own culturally specific traditions while actively making space for other traditions, valuing and learning from them all.

Measuring Success by the Capacity to Care

What would it look like if the expression of care became one of the highest values in our communities? Imagine what the world would be like if care in the form of kindness, compassion, mutuality, and empathy was held up as the ultimate measure of success. Businesses often measure success narrowly, by transactional metrics such as the company's quarterly earnings. What if relational metrics were equally important measures of success, for example, how comfortable employees feel to express themselves freely in the workplace?

The founder of Alamo Drafthouse Cinema, Tim League, uses metrics of care within the company as a way of defining success. In 1998, Tim and his wife, Karrie, started what is now a chain of cinemas that changed the cinematic experience by serving dinner and drinks during the movie. The company is obsessed with creating an environment where film is taken seriously, and they are famous for prohibitions against talking, texting, and arriving late. "We have one simple rule," says Tim. "If you talk or text during a movie, we kick you out." Their mission of protecting the moviegoing experience has won the company an abundance of fans.

I reached out to Tim after seeing the outdoor amphitheater at Community First! Village and was curious about his experience with the village. "The community cinema idea was really just a goofy idea," he explained. "I met Alan years ago, and he is very open to goofy ideas. I value working with him and supporting that organization."

Tim first became interested in compassionate ways to address the problem of homelessness after his first Alamo Drafthouse Cinema relocated to a downtown spot near the ARCH, the primary resource center and shelter for Austin's homeless residents. Near the ARCH are throngs of people lying on the sidewalk, and because of this some downtown business owners view it as a failure.

Tim walked by the ARCH every day on his way to work, and he developed a greater understanding of the enormity of the challenges faced by people who are homeless. Wanting to be proactive and part of a positive solution, Tim immersed himself in learning about organizations that were trying to alleviate homelessness, and that is when he came across Alan Graham. He found the idea of Community First! Village to be novel and exciting, and he bought into its vision for community.

Tim explained how engaging with Community First! Village has changed his perspective: "I think about my relationship with people who are homeless in Austin. In some ways, not that much has changed. The ARCH is still overflowing. We haven't solved homelessness by any stretch of the imagination. But my perspective has changed tremendously. Before hanging out with Alan, I had a stance of nonengagement [with the homeless] and some level of fear. I didn't make eye contact. Since my involvement with Community First! Village, I see a big, positive change. Now every time I see someone who is homeless, I lead with empathy and understand my privilege."

We discussed the lack of strong familial supports for many people who end up on the streets, and how, once you are homeless, it is overwhelmingly difficult to get back on your feet. Before Alamo Drafthouse, Tim and Karrie's first cinema in Austin went under. "It is not lost on me that I was able to take risks in my life because I had a support network," Tim said. "When our first movie theater went south, I knew I had family support where I could dust myself off and start over again. That is a very important safety net."

The idea of creating community has always been a core value of Alamo Drafthouse. "Our motto is 'Do the right thing, foster community, boldly go, and give a shit,'" Tim explained. "There are two communities really. There's the community of our staff. And we have always looked at the theater as a community gathering place for people who love to watch movies."

As the company grew and increased the number of locations, they began using an online employee engagement platform called Workify as a tool of communication and connection with employees. Workify allows any employee to submit a question or comment to Tim, which can be either anonymous or attached to their name. Tim reads every submission. "Even if anonymous, it allows me to respond directly to that individual human being," he said.

I asked him if he viewed anonymity as helpful or a barrier to fostering open communication. Tim replied, "If someone is going to call me names, it helps that it is anonymous. When I answer five or six of those angry comments, I come to understand that anonymity allows you to be raw. I understand it as passion. They feel that we are not living up to our values or our mission and they are mad about it. I sort of sift through the anger to get to the root of the problem."

Though anonymity makes self-disclosure easier, especially to a boss, it is less likely to help us learn to skillfully talk about our differences. To that point, Tim responded: "We are a company that likes measuring things. And one of the metrics of success is the rate of comments that are not anonymous. Raise that metric and it's a better conversation, usually a more civil [one]. Usually, the first one is not civil, but if I respond back in a meaningful way and address what is the root of the anger, I get a different kind of response. Like, 'I'm talking to a real human being who cares. Sorry about using the f-bomb.'"

I asked him about the challenges of nurturing a culture of care within the company as it expanded into locations across the country. "I came very cautiously to the idea of growth," he said. "We didn't really grow that much in the first ten years. But once I saw the success we were having in Austin with smaller, independent films that we love, I began to ask myself 'How can this be duplicated within a larger company? How can we build localized communities around the country?' That became my personal, primary drive, supporting smaller, independent films by bringing them to more communities. I want the moviegoing community to be excited about discovering new kinds of films.

"It's important to me that there is always room for local, creative initiatives that are community specific. . . . And for me, personally, if I can't find time to immerse myself in movies, then I have made a catastrophic error."

Tim believes that for a young adult without family responsibilities it would be ideal to live in a place like Community First! Village. "Just the idea of so many gathering spaces interspersed throughout the single-occupancy houses. It probably would be too expensive as a general way to build community, but what a concept. As opposed to the norm, the more efficient way, which is high-rise apartment living with *no* sense of community."

What if we used variations of this model in thinking about how to meet both the housing crisis and the belonging crisis in this country? If community were viewed as the best incubator for healthy belonging, then any development that discourages it is in my view too costly.

Alan's invitation for Tim to bring his novel and quirky ideas to the village became a way to draw the larger Austin community into the fold as neighbors. If most creative brainstorming was similarly community-centered, it would be a game changer, fundamentally transforming the way we relate to each other.

the vulnerable help us shed our masks

Love and suffering walk hand in hand. If you try to get too far away from one, you also get away from the other.

—BEN NOLAN, L'ARCHE COMMUNITY LEADER

When we are accepted for who we are, and we feel safe and free to show ourselves without masks, we belong to a community unconditionally. There are two essential things we need in order to experience ourselves as being an integral part of a community. The first is a recognition that we are valued and have gifts to share that the community needs. Second, just as we have unique gifts, we also have unique challenges for which we need to receive community acceptance and support. Not all our strengths and talents are immediately visible, and the same is true for our struggles and vulnerabilities. Vibrant communities make accommodations so everyone can participate meaningfully.

Unfortunately, in this culture of ingrained ableism, vast amounts of human creativity and resources are untapped, and nowhere is this more evident than for people with disabilities.

In this chapter you will meet L'Arche, a worldwide community that is quietly countercultural. By adapting to the needs of all its members, it embodies acceptance in simple yet powerful ways. In L'Arche homes, people who have been shut out of the mainstream due to intellectual disabilities teach others how to live in radical connection. They are a wonderful model of a community creating relationships across differences, one of the most pressing and important undertakings of our time.

Reimagining Community One Home at a Time

L'Arche's core values of acceptance, inclusion, and mutuality create the conditions of belonging for those who struggle to find a place in mainstream ableist society. Its mission is to raise awareness of the gifts of people with intellectual disabilities and to advocate with them on their behalf. It fulfills its mission beautifully in more than 150 individual homes spanning forty-five countries on five continents, where people with and without intellectual disabilities share life together. More than anything, L'Arche is a model for how to build close relationships that change the way we see the world and relate to each other.

In the United States each L'Arche community is a regional nonprofit that has one or more homes and is affiliated with the umbrella L'Arche USA organization. Each home has roughly an equal number of people with and without developmental disabilities, depending upon the needs of the individuals and the size of the house. For example, I visited a home in the greater Washington, DC, L'Arche community in which nine people lived: four people with disabilities, four assistants, and a house leader. In addition, another assistant is present overnight in case someone is needed when everyone else sleeps. The house is large enough to also accommodate an overnight guest.

Currently there are nearly twenty L'Arche communities in the United States, more densely clustered on the East Coast and in the Midwest. There are also several new L'Arche communities emerging. Sometimes a new community is started or a home is built by families who join together with a dream of creating a loving, inclusive community for an adult child with a developmental disability. L'Arche communities occasionally expand over time to include additional homes. For example, in the L'Arche community of greater Washington, DC, there are currently four homes, with plans for another in Arlington County, Virginia. The community is partnering with Habitat for Humanity of Northern Virginia in converting a historic farmhouse into a new L'Arche home.

● ● ●

People with intellectual disabilities are *core members,* forming the heart of L'Arche homes and of the organization itself. Intellectual disabilities have many causes, including genetic syndromes such as Down syndrome or fragile X syndrome, an illness such as meningitis or measles, or exposure to toxins such as mercury.[1] Developmental disabilities are a broader category that include chronic disabilities that can be cognitive, physical, or a combination of the two.

People with intellectual disabilities often have below-average cognitive abilities as well as significant challenges in performing everyday activities like self-care, communicating, and socializing. While these disabilities impact developmental milestones such as speaking, walking, and being able to care for one's own personal needs, early intervention and education enable adults with intellectual abilities to lead a meaningful life in a supportive community.

The disabilities that L'Arche community members have can impact conversation, both verbalization and listening comprehension. While the experience of everyone with an intellectual disability is different, what core members have in common is their ability to connect and actively communicate, including those who do so in more nonverbal ways.

When people encounter L'Arche, they sometimes have difficulty expressing what makes it so unique and how personal transformation happens within the community. Yet its message is simple and powerful: "Spend time with people who are different from you, people you have considered other, and you will be transformed," explained Tina Bovermann, national leader and executive director of L'Arche USA.

Before coming to live at L'Arche, most of the core members have had personal experiences of marginalization. After arriving, they are highly valued participants in homes, as well as within the larger organization. In fact, disabled people are the ambassadors who welcome others to share in this community.

The assistants who live with core members—often, but not always, young adults—commit to live at least one year in a home. All members share household responsibilities such as cooking meals and doing dishes, while assistants also provide direct care for core members. Being a L'Arche assistant is far more than a job; the assistants take part in socializing, celebrating, and everything else that makes sharing life together meaningful.

When talking about their experience at L'Arche, assistants often use the word *family*. They view the community as a place of home and safety, where you are accepted for who you are, just as you are. People who have lived in a L'Arche home say it was a time of growth, and it shaped their life choices moving forward.

Although many assistants move on after a year or two, some return to the organization in different capacities after having other life experiences. For example, senior leaders often began as assistants. The organization encourages individuals to take time to reflect on their vocation before returning to L'Arche so that continuing in a different capacity is a source of growth, not stasis.

* * *

L'Arche has diversity at the heart of its mandate, though as with so many communities, it has unfinished work to do. The majority of its membership is Christian, middle class, and white. They have made greater inroads in diversity around spiritual and sexual identities than they have with racial diversity. There is more diversity among its core members than among the other community members.

In 2019, L'Arche USA, the umbrella organization in the United States, adopted a five-year mandate of building greater diversity. The homes in the communities across the country created teams to strategize how to be more inclusive not only of people with disabilities but of underrepresented groups in general.

L'Arche USA is serious about including people with developmental disabilities at every level. Core members participate in organizational reflections, decision-making, revisions to the organization's goals, and implementation of its mission. L'Arche USA holds regional gatherings in which all members participate in the community beyond their personal homes. Every five years, representatives from every home take part in envisioning how to move forward as an organization. Core members are an essential part of this process.

It takes considerable time and resources to have so many people involved with planning at this level, and some might see it as inefficient. Yet this kind of grassroots participation ensures that the goals adopted at these gatherings take root.

* * *

Nowhere will you find a greater intermingling of the mundane and the celebratory aspects of day-to-day life than in L'Arche. The requirements of daily living for people with disabilities are sometimes substantial. Yet because they are met in the context of loving and accepting relationships, these same requirements can offer poignant moments of connection.

While the needs of core members vary from person to person, assistants provide direct care in areas such as personal care needs and skill building, money management, medical care, transportation, and connection to work and family. While assistants are not medical personnel, they have been trained in first aid, administering medication, and recognizing certain medical conditions.

Except during the COVID-19 pandemic, most core members leave the house during the day to participate in a day program or supported employment initiative. These programs provide structure, and they offer skill building and a chance to build community outside the homes.

In nearly all L'Arche homes, part of the daily routine includes preparing meals, eating, and cleaning up together. Dinner is a significant community meal; people take their time and visit with each other, and guests are sometimes invited. On weekends, members from two or more homes in the same community might come together for a larger gathering.

L'Arche is serious about having fun, and few communities could hold a candle to their creative ways of celebrating. Birthdays are special occasions when the entire house joins in honoring the member making another trip around the sun. The person in charge of planning the celebration organizes others to bake the cake, make the card, decorate, and shop for a gift. During the festivities, house members and invited guests might join in a circle to share what the birthday person means to them.

Playfulness, singing, spontaneous dance parties, and belly laughs are part of daily life. Members from different homes in the same community sometimes join for adventures such as bowling, eating out, and barbecues. They take trips together, renting a beach house or traveling to a national park. Some swap houses with other L'Arche communities because it can be challenging to find disability-accessible places for getaways.

One night, a L'Arche home in Washington, DC, invited me to join them for dinner at a restaurant. Nine of us went to one of their favorite pizza places. While we were seated, one of the core members walked around the table pushing empty chairs into new locations, which seemed to put her more at ease. The rest of our group settled into their seats and made space for her to do what felt right to her before she sat down, and the other diners in the restaurant seemed not to notice the commotion.

While everyone was settling in and looking at menus, I looked up and saw that our entire group was swaying to the background music. We were in a sort of connected, synchronized, seated dance that was happening beneath our conscious awareness. I turned to Bruce Weaver, a core member sitting beside me, who looked me in the eyes, smiled, and giggled. It was as if he recognized what was going through my mind and was acknowledging it.

These moments of connection, of grooving together in ways unspoken, characterize time spent in a L'Arche community.

Celebrating Everyone's Gifts

A core tenet of L'Arche's philosophy is that everyone has gifts to share, including people with intellectual disabilities. However, theirs have been largely overlooked, and L'Arche is a platform that showcases them.

While staying a couple of nights at one of the four L'Arche homes in Washington, DC, I had the chance to experience the community's hospitality firsthand. There most of the core members have language proficiency that allows for back-and-forth conversation. Our time together was spent getting to know each other in a small group, with brief one-on-one moments together. In this setting I sometimes had difficulty understanding people's patterns of speech, similar to when we're trying to track a group conversation with people whose accents are unfamiliar to our ears.

Charles Clark, a resident in the home and a remarkably sprightly man in his eighties, is an advocate for people with disabilities. He has made presentations to local governmental agencies, calling on them to provide more services to this population. Charles is curious, asks questions, and is an attentive listener.

Also living in the home is Laurie Pippenger, who has a wonderful sense of humor and likes to good-naturedly tease the other community members. She loves to dance, and even while making herself a cup of tea or cooking for others (Laurie is known for her cooking), she sashays in the kitchen and moves her hands gracefully. She uses a loom to create beautiful woven objects. Laurie also enjoys knitting, and during the COVID-19 pandemic she led an online knitting class.

Both Charles and Laurie advocated for people with disabilities to have priority in receiving the earliest coronavirus vaccines. At the height of the pandemic, intellectual disability was the second-greatest risk factor for death from COVID-19, right behind old age.

Bruce Weaver, whom we met earlier, has an infectious smile and the capacity to make you feel appreciated simply by the way his eyes rest on you.

I did not get to know resident Francene Short because she preferred to spend time relaxing in her room when I was getting to know the others. She was friendly during dinner, though not so interested in interacting with the new person. Francene was a good model of self-care and setting personal boundaries within a community setting.

• • •

In February 2022, several years after my visit to L'Arche in Washington, DC, Charles was hospitalized, and someone from the L'Arche community was at his side every minute of his stay. In March he returned home, where he was placed in hospice care. He recognized that others in the house would be impacted: "I know they'll be sad and don't want to hear the news." As of this writing, he hopes he still has a long time to live, but "when it's time I want to be ready," he said.

The L'Arche communities in greater DC and beyond rallied around Charles, sending cards as he requested and signing up to visit. Many people have told Charles the impact his friendship has had on them and their community. Friends of L'Arche either brought meals to the house or had them delivered because the assistants, in their support for Charles, now had less time for daily routines.

I spoke with Charles via Zoom, and he shared his thoughts about community, what it meant to him, and also his impact on it. Sarah Moore, a dear friend of Charles's who works in a leadership role at L'Arche, joined us on the call and provided additional information about what Charles shared. For example, she fleshed out ways in which Charles was seen as a leader in his home and the larger L'Arche community. Sarah was able to talk to Charles about his health and the resulting recent changes in his life in a knowledgable, sensitive way.

Sarah asked Charles what he wanted as his legacy. One thing stood out for him: he wants to be known as an advocate, both for the L'Arche organization and for people with disabilities in general. He also wants there to be more L'Arche homes so that everyone has the opportunity to live in one.

I asked Charles how he advocates for people with disabilities. "I try to get Medicaid waivers," he explained. "People with disabilities need Medicaid waivers to join L'Arche. . . . I've been on Capitol Hill too. . . . And I recruit people. I go to colleges where students are going to graduate, and I give a speech: 'Come to L'Arche.'"

Sarah added that even if people qualify for assistance, there aren't enough funds for them all, so there is often a waiting list. Charles has been a forceful advocate for others to have access to the same support he has. She shared that Charles is an avid reader of the *Washington Post,* staying on top of disability-related issues. The ARC of Northern Virginia, an advocacy group for people with disabilities, partners with L'Arche by filtering information and letting them know how they can help. Charles always says yes to whatever needs to be done.

Regarding Charles's skill as a recruiter, Sarah shared two examples of women who came as summer volunteers and then continued as assistants because of his caring and persuasive influence. She said to Charles, "You have a remarkable way of bringing people together, making them feel like they belong to you, and that they belong in relationships."

Charles also wants to be known as someone who brings love and peace to his community. He offered examples of how love and peace are shared in the house: "We hug each other. And we help each other a lot, you know? . . . Everybody is together, and all of us are brothers and sisters."

Although Charles is in hospice, he intends on living fully and has more things to accomplish. He wants to continue to represent L'Arche to the outside world, travel, and fish. The weekend after we spoke, two L'Arche assistants were joining Charles on a fishing trip. Charles intended to catch "a great big trout. I'm gonna bring it home and slice it up. Get all the bones [out] so there are no bones. And fry it up for dinner. That would be a good dinner, too."

Charles ended our conversation the same way he has every time we've spoken: he told me he cares about me and suggested that I come for a visit.

●　●　●

Like members of all communities, people in L'Arche sometimes face emotional challenges. Interacting with people who have different preferences, needs, and communication styles can sometimes test our patience. These challenges are part of day-to-day life in any community that lives together, and in most relationships between people who trust and care for each other.

Core members, who generally live in the homes for years, repeatedly experience the loss of a dear friend when an assistant moves on. Being both an assistant and a community member is demanding, and young people in these positions have less time to socialize with others outside the home than other kinds of living situations allow. The monotony of daily routine can get boring, all the more so when members were on lockdown together for an extended period because of COVID-19.

Curt Armstrong came decades ago to work as a young assistant in France, in the home where L'Arche first started nearly sixty years ago. Later he moved up into leadership roles in the organization. He observed that most people in L'Arche can name someone they've had difficulty getting along with in the L'Arche community. It's these challenging relationships within our communities that sometimes provide the greatest opportunity to transform into tenderness and trust.

His experiences living in the first L'Arche home translated into his later work in leadership positions. "The powerful community I experienced in my twenties is still with me now," he said. After working for years in France, he moved with his family back to the United States in 2012 to establish the first L'Arche home in Atlanta, Georgia. There they had the responsibility of representing L'Arche to the larger, surrounding community. "It was stressful because we had to get licensed, find assistants, fundraise, and build a strong board. That was a part of the project, but so was the grace of people with disabilities."

Curt shared his thoughts on some of the challenges and opportunities of creating a community like this in the United States, compared to his experience in France. France provides funding for people with disabilities without the level of bureaucracy that exists in the United States. At the same time, he said that "the entrepreneurial energies in the United States are wonderful. If we can take those energies, and slow down and be more welcoming, everybody benefits. I saw this in Atlanta, where people drove a couple of hours just to visit us. Some of them came because they had a child with a disability. It was remarkable, the synergy and joy . . . that these simple acts generate, creating a powerful common project.

"During my time in Atlanta I learned that L'Arche is a way of being in the world. There's a welcoming of people and a directness that allows building trust. You don't just start with the business at hand; the person across from you matters. And [recognizing this] changes the way the conversation happens."

Curt emphasizes that at its heart L'Arche is about loving relationships, and the core members are wonderful teachers in how to be present to them. "That [directness] is a quality that so many people with disabilities have," Curt said. "I don't know why, and I don't want to romanticize the challenging lived reality of having a disability. But at the same time there is truth to that."

• • •

L'Arche USA is a faith-based community. When representatives are asked if they are a religious organization, their response is that they promote the well-being of each member, regardless of faith, religion, or philosophical tradition. The website of the L'Arche community in Tahoma, Washington, describes faith as "a school of love, with the greatest teachers being our core members. Although each L'Arche community may have different spiritual traditions, all communities are faith communities, rooted in prayer and based in the belief that each person has unique value, and deserves to be loved for who they are."

L'Arche homes often use language and ritual that reflect the predominant faith tradition in the country or region where they reside. In the United States, many homes draw from various Christian denominations; others are interreligious or subscribe to no faith. In the safe space of an accepting, vibrant community, what is most important is that all beliefs and traditions are recognized, honored, and meaningfully incorporated.

L'Arche USA's stated definition of faith reminds me of a retreat talk I once heard by Stephen Batchelor, a Buddhist teacher and author who leads retreats and seminars around the world. He defines faith as a state of care about what matters most, or our ultimate concerns. Raised in a secular family in England, Stephen has at different times considered himself agnostic and atheist, and he is a proponent of secular Buddhism. By "secular" he means that his focus of inquiry is on the living beings on the planet right now, rather than on some possible existence after we die. In his view, being religious isn't about membership in an institution. Stephen considers himself religious as defined by a sensibility of questioning. His questions center upon how to cultivate a life that promotes caring, compassion, and love.

* * *

My first visit to a L'Arche home happened when I was in college, over thirty years ago, when two other college students and I went to Erie, Pennsylvania, over spring break. It was ostensibly an opportunity to spend our holiday in service to others, but I don't believe we were the ones being of service. We were each warmly welcomed into a different home and invited to share the experience of friendship and community.

After spring break was over, I lost contact with the organization, but when the idea of a book on belonging and community called out to be written, I immediately thought of my time there. I reached out to Tina Bovermann, the director of L'Arche USA, and she agreed to speak with me. After our conversation, Tina connected me to people working at L'Arche in both France and in Washington, DC.

When I recall my first visit to a L'Arche home in the late 1980s, my memories are a blur of lingering meals, pitching in with chores, laughter, and connection. For some reason, the only memory that stands out vividly is a brief exchange with Mary, a soft-spoken woman in her sixties whose room I shared. Mary enjoyed reading the newspaper before she went to sleep. As we turned in, she asked if leaving her bedside light on for a time would keep me up. I have no other specific memories of her.

Mary had come to L'Arche after years of living in an institution. Until the 1980s, most physicians recommended that mentally disabled children should be put in these places, despite inhumane conditions and an absence of basic education or health care. The prevailing view was that it was unlikely they would be able to walk or talk, and they certainly could not become valued members of society. People with Down syndrome and other intellectual disabilities were not expected to live beyond their twenties.

Mary's parents did not put her in a facility at first; she spent her childhood at home. But when Mary entered puberty, they worried that she would attract unwanted attention from men. To protect her, they placed her in an institution. She lived there for decades before coming to live in a L'Arche home. Mary didn't like to talk about that time in her life.

My memory of Mary is not part of a larger narrative. It is not emotionally charged; nor is it one I would think to share with others. Maybe the memory remains vivid because the interaction challenged my notions of difference on a visceral level rather than an intellectual one. Whatever the reason, this is the kind of quiet memory that, to me, captures how the moments of connection within a L'Arche home linger.

Disability as Diversity

It is estimated that one in four Americans have a disability, using the definition of a difficulty in one or more of five areas: vision, cognition, mobility, self-care, or independent living.[2] So it is striking that our culture often remains woefully ignorant of the tremendous resources that people with disabilities can bring to the table. I first heard of musician Gaelynn Lea when she was interviewed on Krista Tippett's *On Being* podcast. The winner of NPR's 2016 Tiny Desk contest, Gaelynn was born with brittle bone disease, has never walked, and uses a wheelchair. She plays the violin like a cello because her medical condition makes her limbs tiny and what she describes as "bendy."

After winning the NPR contest, Gaelynn toured full time with the help of her husband and has performed in forty-three states and seven countries. She also cofounded the organization Recording Artists and Music Professionals with Disabilities to amplify disability culture and advocate for greater accessibility in the music business.

Classically trained but best known for her folk-style original music, Gaelynn pushes the boundaries of what can be done with a violin. She also challenges mainstream notions of what can be accomplished with a disability like hers. During interviews she frequently observes how ableism gets in the way of accepting our differences. In her song lyrics, her central message is that life is difficult and beautiful at the same time.

"People think of disability as a negative or as something that they wouldn't want. But it's a really valid way to exist," Gaelynn explained in the *On Being* podcast. "It can create different ways of seeing the world because people with disabilities spend every day modifying everything." Because she can't do most things like everyone else, she is free from having to do things like everyone else.[3]

Gaelynn's disability has enabled her to develop a gift for innovation, rethinking how things are done. She told Krista Tippett, "I wish we can get rid of the stigma and embrace disability as diversity. . . . There's a lot of things that disability has made visible for me but can apply to everyone. We call certain things disabilities or diseases. I just don't see them as compartmentalized things. We are humans, and disability is a part of every single person's life. Some of us just don't identify with it."[4]

Gaelynn knew from a young age that it was futile to try to fit into the mold of what our culture perceives as valuable, beautiful, or cool. "Beauty standards are bogus anyway and trap us," and "all standards are impositions," she said. She came to believe that being invisible to others was preferable to being scrutinized. Free of trying to measure up, she could then focus on things that made her feel beautiful, such as bright-colored dresses and jewelry.[5]

"Of course I had worries: 'Oh, maybe no one will find me attractive, and I won't get married,'" she said. "But I had this freedom to develop into the person I wanted to be without feeling weighed down by these standards that weren't attainable." Freedom is an idea she emphasizes: "The world of capitalist sexuality is designed to make you lose. Because of my disability, I had this freedom right out of the gate. With time, that freedom made me more confident and less weighed down. After that I started dating, but I had to have the realization first. I may have looked left out and sad, but I was actually in this place of intense freedom to be who I was."[6] Still, freedom to be authentic did not always protect her from the pain of marginalization.

People with disabilities have different kinds of needs from people in the mainstream, and in some ways they are more dependent. But Gaelynn pointed out that just because you need physical care doesn't mean you aren't providing care. Several people in the L'Arche community who do not have intellectual disabilities told me about their own initial misperceptions that speak to Gaelynn's point. For example, the assistants often came to live in a L'Arche home because they wanted to be of service to people with cognitive disabilities. But before long they realized that they received just as much, or more, in the way of care.

Gaelynn's message from the margins is that we are free—free to take risks, to be beautiful in the way that feels right to us, and to love who we want to love. Her example, like that of the L'Arche communities, inspires us to let go of society's arbitrary and harmful standards of beauty and worthiness. It is possible to stop trying to live up to an external standard if we prioritize cultivating our most authentic voices and live our lives according to our own measure of what is most important.

Gaelynn's song "I Wait" came to her from feeling left out of the conversation and frustrated that people who claimed to stand up for human rights excluded people with disabilities. It ends with the words, "We need a seat now at the table, so please invite us or don't pretend to care." Gaelynn is hopeful that there will be a shift in perception from perceiving disabilities in a negative light, and that instead we adopt a much larger worldview of the vast range of abilities.

Gaelynn continues to break down barriers for people with disabilities, most recently in her 2022 Broadway musical collaboration. She was tapped by director Sam Gold to compose the haunting musical score for the Broadway version of *Macbeth*.

● ● ●

Our communities should be places where we challenge the ableist mindsets that often operate outside our awareness. By focusing on our own perceptual limitations, rather than on the challenges of people with disabilities, we can better surface and appreciate the gifts of everyone.

Relationships That Challenge Our Perceptions

Perhaps more than the other communities in this book, L'Arche has a subtle magic, but subtlety makes it no less impactful. The communities' superpower may not be immediately obvious to those who don't have the eyes to see it; however, if you spend time in one of the houses, it doesn't take long for a perceptual shift. Curt Armstrong speaks of the power of L'Arche this way: "I came to understand that I needed L'Arche as much as or more than it needed me."

Ben Nolan came to France from England as a young man thirty years ago to be an assistant in La Semence, one of four homes in the village of Trosly-Breuil in the Oise region of France, fifty miles north of Paris. This is where L'Arche got its start back in 1964, when founder Jean Vanier invited two men with intellectual disabilities to come live with him. Ben is now the leader of the L'Arche community in Trosly-Breuil, which also includes two special centers for people with disabilities. La Semence is a home where the core members are profoundly disabled, most do not speak, and all need a high level of assistance.

When asked what initially drew him to L'Arche, Ben responded: "Living a simple life and making the well-being of others as important as my own." However, when Ben first came to La Semence, he did not want to stay. He didn't know the language and felt lost, and the core members' level of handicap seemed too much for him.

But after two days he experienced a transformation in the way he saw people. Instead of seeing their challenges as a barrier, "I was bowled over by the beauty of the people. It is kind of analogous to falling in love, unexpected and difficult to explain. And I couldn't understand how I hadn't seen it before."

He laughed. "I didn't suddenly start wearing new L'Arche glasses and see beauty in everyone. Living with core members is great, but living with volunteers is tough. What draws us together is the gifts of the core members, and those gifts help us get over the difficulties that happen in community."

One of L'Arche's greatest gifts is its insistence that all humans have more to bring to the table than what initially meets the eye. Ben said, "Here, real beauty is revealed, not superficial beauty." Gifts are not centered on "productivity or the capacity to generate wealth." The struggle is then how to fend off amnesia of what we have seen and keep hold of this revelation. "We take off our masks [in L'Arche] but they get pushed back in place when we step outside of community," Ben explained. "Letting go of this image we want to portray to the world can take a lifetime."

• • •

Ben makes an effort to join the community at La Semence for lunch every Friday. He feels fortunate to still have a close connection to the community there, including core members he met when he was a young assistant. When I visited members from the L'Arche organization about an hour outside of Paris, Ben invited me to join him for lunch at La Semence. There, he sat next to Jean-Claude, a core member who not only lived there when Ben first came but was also the best man at Ben's wedding.

People lingered at the table, taking time to connect and catch up with each other. It was a culinary delight befitting a French community, with baked salmon for the main course. Also at the table were four core members, two assistants from other countries, the house leader, and Fred, a neighbor who had been a valued weekly lunch guest for over fifteen years. After the plates were cleared, a tarte aux framboises was brought out, made by Fred's wife.

Initially, I experienced unease at the realities of eating with people with severe disabilities, who at this home have greater needs than the core members in most L'Arche homes. As I heard sounds I was unaccustomed to hearing and sometimes saw food coming out of mouths, I hoped my unease wasn't visible. My discomfort with the unfamiliar soon faded because of everyone else's enjoyment of each other. When Jean-Claude gagged on food and spit it out, the person next to him tenderly and matter-of-factly placed the food in a napkin. Conversation paused only momentarily to see if Jean-Claude was all right; then it quickly started again. The enjoyment of each other's company and the way there was room for everyone's experience were a model of loving community that I will not forget.

Because core members at La Semence aren't able to speak, Ben and other people at the table shared their stories for them. Ben told me about how Jean-Claude loved to ride horses, and after the meal the two of them showed me a picture of a younger Jean-Claude seated atop a horse and smiling. People showed a lot of physical affection toward the core members, who welcomed it, leaned into it, and lit up, nonverbally communicating love and affection in return. The assistants, who all spoke multiple languages, shared their stories of what brought them to L'Arche. Though French is the primary language spoken in the house, much of the conversation was in English for my sake.

● ● ●

L'Arche embodies hospitality, and one of their favorite places to offer it is around the table and over conversation. In Washington, DC, the core members were so welcoming and open, and my time with them made a lasting impact upon me. After two days I felt ready to leave, but I wasn't even an hour into my four-hour drive home to Brooklyn when I felt a pang of missing them.

Charles enjoyed sharing stories of his life and views of community, and he was also curious about my experiences. Bruce was attentive during the conversation and afterward asked if I'd like to go to his room to see his new iPad, and he showed me how he stayed connected with family on it. And I thought of how Laurie put on makeup, danced and sang, and brought a spirit of joie de vivre to the home. I'm grateful to Charles, Laurie, and Bruce for opening my eyes and expanding my capacity to appreciate ability, physicality, and beauty.

In vibrant communities it is easy to envision a different world because there we experience what is possible. At moments it seems so simple—and absurd—how we are conditioned not to clearly see what is before us. At the same time, I appreciate Ben Nolan's insight about how easy it is to slip into amnesia, forgetting what we saw and understood as we live in the world of conditional belonging.

It's important to acknowledge that the gifts of people with intellectual disabilities do not, in any way, minimize their suffering from being marginalized. A truly civilized society does not place people in the margins in the first place. It is also true that the people with disabilities at L'Arche are skilled at building vibrant community. A message I heard repeatedly from members of L'Arche, and the organization's friends, is that core members have a direct way of relating that gets to the heart of acceptance, in part because they don't wear the masks that most of us put on, consciously or not, in our longing to belong.

Grief Plants the Seeds of Renewal

L'Arche founder Jean Vanier died in the spring of 2019 at the age of ninety. Upon his passing, people throughout the world praised his lifelong work of bringing awareness to the gifts of people with cognitive disabilities. His books on community have made an impact on many people all over the world, myself included. In his life he received numerous honors and awards, including a nomination for a Nobel Peace Prize, and some considered him a saint. In Canada, schools were named after him.

Less than a year after his death, findings from a report commissioned by L'Arche's international leadership detailed credible accusations that Vanier had had abusive sexual relationships with six women who had turned to him for spiritual guidance.[7] None of these women had developmental disabilities or were part of the L'Arche community. All these women felt coerced and suffered lasting emotional wounds.

The L'Arche community was rocked with pain, betrayal, anger, and confusion. Many members had had personal relationships with Vanier and considered him a close friend. A man they trusted—who until this revelation had seemed to exemplify a life of treating everyone with dignity and love—had psychologically manipulated women who were vulnerable with him.

Even though Vanier had stepped back from active leadership within the organization decades earlier, L'Arche's identity was intimately tied to its origin story of how he came to found it. When they received the report's findings, the current leadership was fully transparent, standing on the side of truth and of the courageous women who told their stories, and unequivocally condemned his behavior. Core members were told about the abuse with no attempts to sugarcoat what happened. This was a test of L'Arche's ability to move beyond its origin story—a crucial first step in growing as an organization by owning an identity more complex than that story suggests.

Not knowing how to integrate these revelations myself, I initially considered excluding L'Arche from this book, concerned that it would detract from the book's message. But to do so would have been a mistake, because L'Arche homes are vibrant communities that personify the best of what we can be. It also would have been a missed opportunity to explore the need, everywhere, for an honest reckoning with the contradictions that exist within all our traditions and collective origin stories.

No institution is immune from abuses of power, and this is also true for the communities we love. Crises can shine light on unhealthy power structures at the heart of our traditions as they have existed and currently function, deepening our capacity to build vibrant community moving forward. This kind of crisis presents an opportunity to examine how our minds elevate leaders' narratives in a way that is human nature but also contradicts a quality of vibrant community: everyone's stories are an integral part of the fabric. By acknowledging and condemning past harm with an honest accounting of the dynamics of inequity that remain, we are able to build relationships and communities that are truly inclusive, safe, and places of healing for everyone.

Crisis lets in the light and exposes the cracks, often revealing a portal that can lead us to a place of deeper understanding.

L'Arche is beginning the process of coming to terms with its past. The organization's leadership created space for members to grieve—to have their painful experience of betrayal and anger and to integrate that experience. There were plans for a listening tour where leadership would go to L'Arche homes across the country and be present as members shared their feelings and thoughts, but then the COVID pandemic hit, and everyone's lives and plans were upended. Core members were cut off from the outside world, unable to go to their day programs or receive outside visitors.

In L'Arche's 2021 federation leadership meeting to extend the organization's charter, the abuse revelations were directly addressed, naming the grief and loss that the community was experiencing, and articulating the need to integrate this new reality. Out of this process, guidelines, tools and techniques were offered to the individual home communities in order to continue the dialogue.[8]

Despite the tensions, pain, and disruptions of 2020 and beyond, L'Arche remains anchored in its ability to create relationships across differences. Tina Bovermann comments on the silver lining to these devastating revelations: "I'm having so many conversations, and people are rallying around L'Arche. We are growing as individuals and as an organization. Members of L'Arche are asking important questions: 'What is the place of a charismatic leader?' We need to examine how we elevate leaders. And what are the systems in place that require account- ability for all?"

True to the heart of this organization, people with disabilities not only contribute but lead the way. Even while core members experienced their own pain when hearing about the abuse, they loved and supported others with openness and integrity. One core member stayed next to an assistant throughout the day, asking him how he felt after first hearing the news. Another told an assistant, "I'm here for you if you need me."

Laurie from the L'Arche community in Washington, DC, took an assistant's shoulders in her hands and declared, "L'Arche changed my life, so forget him!" And with a flourish, she snapped her fingers.[9]

inclusion is a spiritual practice

Dominator culture has tried to keep us all afraid,
to make us choose safety instead of risk, sameness
instead of diversity.

—BELL HOOKS,
TEACHING COMMUNITY: A PEDAGOGY OF HOPE

In June 2021, L'Arche USA held an online symposium where they looked at the findings of a two-year evaluation of its community based upon member feedback. The virtual gathering was an opportunity to begin a dialogue around the community's strengths as well as the ways in which it needed to grow and change. Pádraig Ó Tuama, an Irish poet and theologian, was invited to host the two-day event. A masterful storyteller and public speaker, he has worked with groups to explore the themes of story, conflict, violence, and their relationship with religion. At the closing, Pádraig offered the L'Arche community and invited guests a poignant phrase as a point of reflection moving forward:

> *In the beginning there were three things:*
> *something that will always remain;*
> *something that needs to grow;*
> *something that should have never been there.*

This meditation is a helpful examination for every community committed to creating an inclusive culture of whole, authentic beings. What are the things about our communities that we most value and want to preserve? When have we not lived up to the values that the group holds? Who have our communities excluded or harmed, intentionally or not? Do we hold conversations in our communities where we ask these kinds of questions?

By looking more clearly at the past and how our origins inform our present, we can better see ourselves. A clear-eyed examination of the strengths and shadows in our communities empowers us to create a better future.

● ● ●

We need to have relationships with people who are different from us—who identify differently, look different, hold different beliefs, and live differently. Diversity expands our understanding of the world and challenges our internal biases. The more diverse a system, the more it makes use of feedback, which, in turn, makes it more complex, creative, and resilient.[1] Diverse systems are open ones, which means they are continuously changing. Our communities are ecological systems; the more inclusive they are, the healthier.[2,3]

We can't become more inclusive without first examining the framework of systemic oppression within our cultural institutions, and by extension, within our personal communities. This makes antiracism and other antibias work an inherent part of inclusion. Within our communities, it is important to have conversations about the layers of both our privilege and our disadvantage and how these impact us. We then need to move beyond conversation to the very hard, ongoing work of implementing real change.

Communities that value and prioritize greater diversity know that making the changes necessary to become more inclusive is ongoing, difficult, and at times painfully slow. Those interviewed for this chapter who are doing the hard work find it to be tremendously important and meaningful. I am uncovering my own blind spots in this area, so I write about the efforts of others doing the same with humility and some hesitancy. Still, if we want to get to a better place, we must start where we are. I hope that describing these efforts to be truly inclusive will help readers do the same within their own communities.

This chapter introduces the reader to two meditation centers where everyone is welcome to participate in their retreats and online offerings. One of these communities is relatively new, and its founding mission is to create a radically inclusive spiritual refuge that is responsive to the needs of the diverse groups that represent the city where it is located. From the beginning it has paid special attention to underrepresented communities. When this center was still only an idea, another one on the East Coast, with a long history of welcoming teachers from many Buddhist traditions but whose membership was predominantly white and middle class, was starting out on the long road to addressing its own barriers to inclusion.

Inclusion Seeds the Ground for a New Consciousness

Having communities where we feel we belong is not only necessary for physical and emotional health; it is also an essential spiritual need. These are the places where we most need to know we are accepted for who we authentically are and to feel that we are represented. If we cannot create more diverse and inclusive spiritual communities, then what are the chances of succeeding on a larger scale? Spiritual communities are places that can make a powerful impact on how we collectively relate to each other, but only if they take seriously the need to dismantle barriers to diversity and inclusion.

It is not enough for these communities to simply refrain from judging, condemning, or rejecting people who don't fit into the dominant narrative. Spiritual communities are vibrant when they move beyond the message that "all are welcome" to active inclusion, representing the stories and experiences of everyone. When true inclusion and equity are practiced in our communities of faith, we strengthen and deepen our spiritual lives.

We cannot have greater racial diversity in our communities without holding the experience of anger and anguish, of grief and trauma, because of centuries of racialized violence and subjugation in our country. When these stories are included and held, so will be those stories about joy and resilience and the heterogeneity within, for example, Black experience.

Similarly, although there have always been gay, transgender, and queer people within faith communities, their stories have been relegated to the margins, often unmentioned. It's important to educate ourselves about the identities represented by the acronym LGBTQIA+ and to learn about various gender identities if we are to welcome diversity and stretch ourselves beyond the straight cisgender narrative. The words represented in the acronym—lesbian, gay, bisexual, transgender and nonbinary, queer, intersex, asexual, and two-spirit—matter because they relate to how someone views themselves, the lifestyle they lead, and how they deserve to be acknowledged by others.

Additionally, as discussed in the previous chapter, if our communities that value equity and justice don't make the effort to create spaces for people with disabilities and diverse abilities to meaningfully participate, then we continue to cause harm under the dominant ableist narrative. Pushing back against ableism includes anything from creating accessible structures to thinking about how meetings are run in the workplace.

Caring about creating the conditions for all people to access the spiritual traditions of their choice *is* the process to creating an inclusive and equitable world.

In Buddhism, as in other faith traditions, teachers often use personal stories along with historical ones to convey the basic teachings. When some members rarely, if ever, hear stories that reflect their own life experiences, they feel excluded—the antithesis of belonging. Although Buddhism has a better track record than other religions when it comes to welcoming differences, particularly those of the LGBTQIA+ community, the bar needs to be raised in all spiritual arenas.

When the dominant group's stories are the only game in town, not only can it trivialize prejudices and discrimination against people who are different; it also mutes their vibrancy and importance to the community. When we elevate everyone's stories as wisdom stories and tear down the margins within our communities, we gain insight about how the experience of privilege has stifled our collective ability to be fully authentic.

● ● ●

Holding conversations where we feel safe, respected, and welcomed for all that we are is a powerful gateway to creating diverse, healthy spiritual communities. Identity is complex, and we contain multitudes; differences in the nuances of how we identify are not always visible or obvious. When our communities are inclusive spaces in which all our stories, including those of our identities, are part of a larger vibrant narrative, they are places of liberation from the biased and sometimes toxic messages we have internalized.

Here are some questions that might be helpful starting points for reflection and conversation. What are the messages we received as children, and as adults, about our identities? Did any of those messages cause us to deny who we are or to feel shame or confusion? Which of our identities give us privilege, and which ones marginalize us? Has the way we've thought about our identities changed over time, and if so, how? Which identities pushed us to grow as humans, and which, if any, impeded our growth? What do we want our communities to understand and be sensitive to about how we identify?

Eastern Buddhism Migrates to the West

Although Buddhism has been practiced in the United States since the early twentieth century, it wasn't until the late 1960s, when Americans traveled to Asia to train with teachers there and then returned to start their own centers, that Buddhism entered the US mainstream.[4] Also at that time, other forms of Buddhism, such as Zen, were taking hold as Asian Buddhist teachers founded their own schools and monasteries in the West. Buddhism is a major world religion, but people don't need to adopt it as their personal religion to benefit from its twenty-five-hundred-year-old spiritual teachings and practices for training the mind.

In 1975 a small group of Western practitioners who had studied Buddhism abroad returned to the United States and founded Insight Meditation Society (IMS) in the rural town of Barre, Massachusetts. Joseph Goldstein, Sharon Salzberg, and Jack Kornfield were at the time young teachers who pooled donations from friends and supporters to buy a former Catholic novitiate in Barre. IMS's mission was to be a spiritual refuge offering the Buddha's teachings and helping practitioners cultivate awareness and compassion in the context of meditation retreats.

Ever since Western Buddhist meditation centers were first founded in this country, their membership has been overwhelmingly middle class and white. As in all homogenous spaces, it is easy to overlook what is specific to the dominant culture and how the cultural environment excludes the experiences of different groups.

Around two decades ago, institutions like IMS began to actively address their lack of diversity when teachers, led by teachers of color, started raising awareness of how the culture's oppressive dynamics were mirrored within their spiritual centers. In addition, new spiritual communities formed that, unlike established centers, had social activism and inclusion as part of their DNA from the outset. A good example of this kind of center is East Bay Meditation Center (EBMC) in Oakland, California.

EBMC, which opened in 2007, is a spiritual center whose mission is radical inclusivity and racial justice work. Welcoming people of color, LGBTQIA+ people, people with disabilities, and people from other underrepresented communities, EBMC offers teachings and practices from Buddhism as well as other spiritual wisdom traditions. Though its mission of radical inclusivity was never questioned, putting that mission into practice is an ongoing challenge, and the community continuously works to undo the many ways in which people are excluded.

Carol Cano, a core teacher at EBMC, brings her Basque and Native American heritage to her spiritual teaching. Her personal experience deepens her understanding of identity's complexity and her appreciation for the challenges and opportunity that EBMC presents. Carol says radical inclusion is a necessary practice for anyone committed to the path of doing no harm:

> There's nothing like it. They really mean inclusion. And what is challenging about it is the intersectionality of so much happening, so many different communities coming together. It was such a process of learning and stretching myself.
>
> [For example] I now understand the fluidity of gender, and I change the language of my dharma talks to reflect greater inclusivity. As a cis woman, there had been a veil of delusion in my not understanding my privilege around that. And understanding my privilege of being an able-bodied person is another example. In guided meditations I used the word sitting, and there are, literally, people who are not able to sit. They bring a folding chair that reclines so that their body can lie down. It took time to change the way I taught, and it required that I see things differently. The effort, which was uncomfortable at first, taught me to understand diversity, to look closely at both the seen and the unseen as a practice.

It's about keeping up with the times of who is showing up in community and how we meet them. It's not just about our personal insight practice. It's learning how to take our personal insight and relate it to others in the community. And that means stretching ourselves in all senses of the word.

● ● ●

Creating a more inclusive and diverse community is about liberation—from a small worldview, from conformity, and from fear of difference. It takes intention, reflection, and a lot of practice for us to viscerally understand the truth that we are strengthened when we welcome difference. Audre Lorde, who described herself as a Black mother, poet, and lesbian, said that our differences don't divide us. On the contrary, what causes division "is our inability to recognize, accept, and celebrate those differences."[5]

Opening to different perspectives liberates us from the illusion that we and those people we view as being like us have the answers or are best equipped to solve complex problems. This is fortunate because interdependence is our reality, and recognizing this fact is the only thing that will save us from the existential challenges we face.

DaRa Williams, a clinician and core meditation teacher at IMS, takes a wide view, asserting that diversity is one critical step, but it is not the end goal of radical inclusion. "There needs to be an entire shift in perception, understanding, and awareness around access and power," she explained. As long as we resist this shift and cling to categories and hierarchies, we will continue to suffer in the realm of conditional belonging that threatens our very existence. Resisting change limits our vision of what can be, especially because exclusion and separateness are at the heart of what ails us as humans and the planet.

A Buddhist Center Examines Its History of Exclusion

IMS offers opportunities for silent meditation retreats in lengths ranging from days to several months. The society practices the ancient Vipassana tradition of meditation. Vipassana means "to see clearly," and practitioners of this tradition use meditation to observe states in the body and mind as they are happening. They learn techniques to settle their thoughts, enabling them to gain insight into the nature of their minds and their lives. The IMS meditation retreats are designed to deepen personal insight practices and anchor them in everyday life. The retreats are held in silence except for an evening dharma talk. In Buddhism, the term *dharma* means the truth that is universal to everyone. A community of people who practice the dharma together is referred to as a *sangha*.

Joseph Goldstein, one of IMS's founders, reflected on how the organization awakened to the fact that lack of diversity was an issue they needed to address.[6] At first it felt normal to have a space with few people of color; "it didn't occur to us that this was a problem," he said. "We thought, 'Why would someone not feel safe?'"

But later he and others realized that being one of the "two to three people of color with a hundred white folks does not create a feeling of safety. And that was a revelation for us. . . . It's kind of shocking that there was so much cluelessness."

Joseph's reflection highlights how we can only gain insight where we shine the light of inquiry. We can't make change until we first identify what needs changing within ourselves and our communities. This insight means reckoning with our past and flexing an awareness muscle that many of us have yet to more fully develop. Thanks to the enduring efforts of teachers of color, like Gina Sharpe and DaRa Williams, IMS has remained focused on dismantling racism and other forms of exclusion within the sangha.

Gina Sharpe led early efforts at IMS to offer retreats specifically to those who self-identified as people of color (POC). The organization addressed barriers to attendance, such as establishing a scholarship program so all who were interested would be able to afford the retreat. Gina—who is also a cofounder of New York Insight, an urban mindfulness center in Manhattan—introduced the Black, Indigenous, and people of color (BIPOC) community in New York City to IMS.

The POC retreats were led in teams, with at least one teacher self-identifying as a person of color. Teaching in teams is an effective way to redistribute the power dynamics in places that are predominantly white. These retreats are now taught only by teachers of color, who also lead the general retreats and hold leadership positions within the organization.

When the dharma is taught and shared by people with a broad range of backgrounds and experience, it deepens the knowledge base of the dharma for everyone. Greater diversity among the teachers is not only beneficial for retreat participants of color; it also transforms the experience for white practitioners who have previously been taught only by teachers they experienced as being like them.

In addition to the POC retreats, IMS introduced affinity groups within the general retreats, which are smaller groups that meet during one or more of the daily meditation periods. These smaller groups are available to people who identify as POC and LGBTQIA+, groups that have a history of underrepresentation in the community. These offerings are optional, and not everyone who qualifies wishes to join. The people who do participate find them beneficial as a source of ease during the general retreats, helping them feel more connected to the larger IMS community.

Some participants in the general retreats are uncomfortable with these affinity groups, feeling they perpetuate a sense of separateness within the community. But the IMS leadership believes the sangha supports all its members in an important way by providing safe spaces for those who have not always experienced safety in the larger community there. These affinity groups are an acknowledgment that nondominant groups have borne, and continue to bear, a burden from cultural insensitivities in homogenous venues.

DaRa Williams said the POC retreats were an essential refuge that helped deepen her own spiritual practice: "I didn't have to engage with microaggressions and tensions that are sometimes experienced as a person of color in a predominantly white space."

● ● ●

Beyond changes to the retreats themselves, an investment at every level of the organization was needed. Rebecca Bradshaw, a senior teacher who sits on IMS's diversity committee, believes this is often not understood when people begin the work of inclusion. "It takes so much more than diversity workshops," she explained. "IMS first had to diversify its board, with at least one-third of the board being people who identified as POC. There needs to be a large enough group for comfort and power." She continued:

> Once we [got diversity on the board] the decisions coming out of it reflected a greater understanding. Then we needed diverse teachers. You can't have diversity if you don't have people at the front representing. We just graduated fifteen [of twenty in the class] teachers who identify as POC. That feels like a completion of a very significant step, an important change happening in the dharma community.
>
> The process leading up to this four-year teacher training took years of preparation to become a reality. In 2013 there was a very important three-month retreat where one-third of the practitioners identified as POC. A lot of people from New York City came, and that was planned. And out of that group came a number of teachers.
>
> There also needs to be greater representation among the staff, and not only line staff but the higher-level administrative staff. That is something that we haven't done well. IMS is located in a very white area that is not very inviting to POC folks. For example, there have been racial incidents walking in the neighborhood.

Becoming more inclusive requires transparency and a system that not only welcomes feedback but actively seeks it out, even feedback that is difficult to hear. It means creating systems of accountability at all levels of the organization. And it requires learning skills for open and honest communication, like holding tension and conflict, which will be discussed in the next chapter.

Many attempts at diversity do not bear fruit because they aren't undertaken with a tangible plan and an ongoing commitment to stay at it. When becoming more welcoming is not partnered with a necessary perceptual shift, the invitation is conditional. Rebecca points out that even the word *welcoming* can be problematic. "The word often means 'we welcome you,' which is part of the problem with communities who are predominantly white trying to become multicultural," she explained. "The whole thinking needs to be changed from 'we are welcoming you to our community' to 'we are creating a community together.'"

Rebecca believes that this work can only be done when we adopt a fundamental perceptual shift. "The problem is that people think they are *supposed to* do this work." That is, when we take action from a perceived "should" or from an abstract sense of duty, we aren't motivated by a sense of empathy and connection. "As long as white people don't have their own emotional understanding of the pain inflicted by racism, they are going to be worried about what is or isn't in it for them," she said. "The heart has to be transformed into seeing and clearly understanding the pain of marginalized people for inner compassion to be ignited. When our compassion is ignited, there is a desire for change."

She continued: "The other understanding that is often missed is how white people suffer under racism. I don't think most white people are consciously aware of how much we have lost in terms of belonging to humanity. The pain of what was lost [is experienced] unconsciously and there is a wish to avoid it. [The pain] can come up for white people as resentment: 'Why do they get special treatment?' But what they are really saying is, 'I want to belong, and I don't belong.'

"By buying into white domination and control, which is the basis of white supremacy, we choke ourselves," Rebecca observed. "When we grieve, we soften ourselves. To do antiracism work, you have to be willing to have your heart broken."

By participating in a system of dominance and privilege, white culture has carved itself out of belonging to a greater humanity, with devastating consequences. To belong to the world in a psychically healthy way, those groups whose ancestors caused harm that continues to this day must acknowledge the past (and present) and make amends. Only when we face conditions as they exist can we grieve, which is an important first step to healing and experiencing true belonging.

• • •

Diversity work takes time because for it to succeed, trusting relationships must be built first. At IMS the years of continued effort have borne fruit, and momentum is building. The POC retreats remain popular, and the general retreats are more diverse as well. For example, in an online retreat in late 2020, there were twenty people of color out of one hundred retreatants, whereas in the past there had been just a few. Besides more people of color in the general retreats, more diverse teaching staff allow all sangha members the benefit of receiving the teachings in fresh ways. When there is substantially greater diversity in the people who teach and attend retreats, a sense of safety, relief, and joy is felt by all, not just practitioners of color.[7]

The new guiding teachers who identify as BIPOC are diverse along various dimensions. They come from different parts of the country as well as from different countries. Unlike many of the senior teachers who have always taught the dharma as their primary vocation, many of the recent graduates worked in other professions before they trained as spiritual guides.

DaRa Williams—who has worked in the mental health field for as long as she has practiced meditation, which she started long before she began teaching—looks forward to seeing how the dharma will grow with these new teachers, and what new communities they will access. "IMS and Spirit Rock [another Buddhist spiritual center on the West Coast] both graduated twenty new teachers, so there are now forty people in two classes where they are mostly BIPOC," she said. "In this wave of graduates, some will choose to teach in more traditional places, centers like IMS. But some of them are wanting to engage more people at every stratum, like teenagers and even younger children and people in prison. And caregivers—that is a community that is not able to go to a retreat for a week. And new parents and single moms certainly have difficulty finding time to go on retreat."

These developments affirm the dharma's future in creating communities filled with strength and resilience *because* of their greater diversity. In the two and a half millennia that the Buddha's teachings have been around, their core wisdom has remained intact while the practices have been adapted to the needs of the different countries to which they spread.

The people at IMS doing the hard work of inclusion will tell you it has become an integral part of their spiritual practice. As they persist in it together, it gets easier. Uncomfortable conversations aren't quite as uncomfortable, and they are less likely to be avoided.

"When we say things that are hurtful, we can hear [about our mistakes] without taking things so personally," says Rebecca Bradshaw. And she adds, "I see a shift in myself; it feels refreshing. To me it is heart opening to recognize my conditioning as a white person, where I can take complete responsibility without collapsing into shame."

* * *

The dharma is practiced to attain enlightenment, which is not an esoteric goal; it means living in a clearer and more uplifting way. Inclusive communities aid us on that path because as we surround ourselves with a wide variety of perspectives, our awareness expands. Radical inclusion in spiritual communities is essential for finding ways to end the suffering caused by greed, hatred, and delusion, the three poisons of the mind according to Buddhist tradition.

Finding Our Blind Spots

Like people who practice other faith traditions, Western Buddhists have only relatively recently recognized that racism is part of entrenched patterns within their communities, often in the form of unrecognized privilege. Although even the most homogenous communities generally do not intend to make people feel unwelcome, their lack of cultural sensitivity is oppressive to those who don't belong to the majority culture.

The act of opening up our language and changing the way we do things so we encourage inclusion does not detract from a community's mission. On the contrary, it has the opposite effect, opening us to a greater sense of belonging.

DaRa Williams explained it this way: "A lot of people still miss that even though they are not consciously, personally racist, systemic oppressions exist in which they participate—whether racism or genderism or homophobia or other oppressions. These are systemic structures existing within our communities, which don't allow people to actualize themselves. They prevent people from accessing what everyone wants to access—love, food, shelter, the ability to make a living.

"White people are just as damaged by the experience of oppression ... in different ways, but just as damaged. We have not reckoned with this in our culture. If America could realize its real dream [of equality and self-actualization], wow, imagine what this place could be like.

"Given that the dharma has been around for two thousand six hundred years, I don't think there is anything that we can do or say that is going to break it up," DaRa said. Her words are relevant for all communities of faith that resist healthy change in the name of tradition.

In every country where Buddhism has migrated, it has been reinvented while the core teachings have remained intact. It follows that the practice of the dharma within the United States, which is still in its infancy, will also change to meet the needs of its communities.

● ● ●

Even among those who desire greater diversity and who understand that we must undo unjust systems, there can be a tendency to view the problem as "out there" and resist doing the hard work on ourselves and within our communities. For example, difficult and necessary discussions are sometimes avoided in order to preserve surface-level peace and harmony. John Welwood, a clinician and Buddhist practitioner, coined the term *spiritual bypassing* to describe this phenomenon of using the idea of enlightenment to rise above the messy side of being human before first fully facing it.[8] The general avoidance of tension and conflict is a hazard of many communities and is not unique to Buddhism and other spiritual centers.

Spiritual bypassing impedes individual and community growth. More problematic still, when spiritual bypassing denies the harm that marginalized groups experience, it prevents us from taking responsibility to do something about it. When we continue to avoid examining how oppressive structures are present within our communities, we are actively participating in the oppression.

A core concept in Buddhist teachings is *anattā,* the idea that the sense of self is delusional and that clinging to our notions of self is a major source of suffering. Reflection on this teaching helps us develop an understanding of how our minds categorize things in ways that cause us harm. But it can also be used as an objection to the work of inclusion (or at least a way of voicing resistance to it, though that resistance may stem more from discomfort). Resistance might look like the questions, "If the dharma is for everyone, why should we have special retreats for certain identities? Isn't that a form of delusion that separates us?"

The suggestion that another's person's experience of identity is illusory is a way of shutting down conversation and dismissing their experience, even if unintended. When anattā, a teaching tool for personal growth, is misapplied, it can be used to silence someone who is different. This misapplication of anattā also denies the reality that there is ample room for the expression of identities of those who represent the majority.

Indeed, although we have widely different backgrounds and experiences, our human needs are remarkably similar. At the same time, external conditions, shaped by our identities, impact our lives in ways that are very real. Those who argue that race is a delusional social construct—and they're right, it is—often fail to recognize the devastating consequences that result from this pervasive, toxic delusion. The privileges and suffering disproportionately experienced by some communities, and sometimes subgroups within our communities, should be of the utmost concern to us all.

It would be incredible to live in a world where race, gender identity, sexuality, and other kinds of socially constructed identities didn't matter, but that is not the world we live in now. When our communities stop relegating the experiences of some of their members to the margins, they can do a better job of dismantling discrimination and prejudice.

● ● ●

When communities do the work of inclusion, especially by holding difficult conversations, discussion opens around other often-avoided topics. For example, there are now more conversations about use and abuse of power by spiritual teachers, including sleeping with their students, asking them for money, or having them work for the teacher for free under the auspices of spiritual training.[9]

In too many faith traditions, students don't feel free to speak up about abuse, and the community sees signs that it ignores or unconsciously blocks from its awareness. In instances when abuse has been revealed, there has been an unfortunate pattern where the community is dismayed or shocked, but then time passes with no effort to examine and address the root causes.

Unhealthy power hierarchies and the resulting abuses that occur in spiritual traditions are no different from those that occur in other institutional settings, and there is an unspoken taboo against speaking out. When a teacher's words are transformative in students' lives, such teachers can be elevated, even deified. When a teacher or spiritual guide's behavior is discovered to be manipulative or abusive, the community has difficulty dealing with the resulting disappointment, sometimes experiencing it as traumatic. One way of dealing with it psychically is denial, where it gets pushed to the unconscious, and those who speak up experience negative consequences.

Vibrant communities must be clear-eyed about the role of teachers, explicitly creating boundaries around what is acceptable and unacceptable behavior, especially the behavior of those in leadership roles.

When we accept that we all have a part to play in changing how power is wielded in our communities, and we actively work to upend unhealthy hierarchies, then we create the conditions for healthy belonging. Vibrant communities recognize that they need to do a better job of drawing clear boundaries and instituting an accountability process for unacceptable behavior, one that includes ample support and validation for those who courageously speak up.

True inclusion requires that we fundamentally perceive and enact power differently, ceding it and sharing it. Perhaps it's more accurate to say that what is needed is a perceptual shift around power, from "power over" to "power with."

• • •

People in the diversity and antiracism space for any length of time emphasize that the work is iterative, and progress often feels glacially slow. Mistakes happen, bad habits can be tenacious and pop up in new ways, and insensitivities can reemerge. I asked DaRa Williams her thoughts on the pace of change at IMS. "It's frustrating at times," she said, "but it's not particular to diversity. It's part of the institutional system where, regardless of any call for change that gets put in front of it, the process is slow and includes resistance."

Only when we stay at it and in it, together, working with and through our pain, tension, and resistance, can we build more insightful, loving, and resilient communities.

Compassion Breaks and Opens the Heart

Thich Nhat Hanh, a Vietnamese monk, peace activist, and beloved spiritual leader, said compassion is born from understanding the suffering of others.[10] The English word *compassion* stems from the Latin roots *com* and *pati,* meaning "to suffer with," and it is not just a feeling; it is empathy in action. Practicing compassion toward ourselves and others is necessary in order to work toward a more just and equitable society.

For example, compassion helps us appreciate when a group of people need to gather and heal separately from the larger community to feel safe and gain empowerment. Compassion requires that we open our hearts to the pain caused by the violence inherent in our systems of dominant culture to the bodies and psyches of people harmed by it. And compassion calls us to look into our hearts and examine resistance to letting go of our privilege.

Self-compassion is recognizing that we, too, are worthy of compassion, and it involves extending to ourselves the same kindness and regard that we extend to people we care about. Self-compassion is active, not complacent. It helps to be kind to ourselves while still taking responsibility when we don't live up to our values. Conditioned by a racist, patriarchal society, we will make mistakes as we work to recondition ourselves. Acknowledging this doesn't excuse us when we are insensitive, prejudiced, or cause harm. It recognizes that we are imperfect, though still capable of owning our mistakes and doing things differently. When we are compassionate toward ourselves, we are more resilient and have more emotional resources to continue to work toward the change that will heal us.

For people harmed by oppressive systems, self-compassion provides some protection from the damaging psychological impact. Studies find that the experience of self-compassion is a protective factor against depression and self-criticism among people who are the targets of racism and other forms of bias and stigma.[11-13] The pain and trauma experienced from marginalization can impair a person's ability to experience self-compassion. For those who struggle with extending compassion to themselves, the good news is that it can be learned through practice, like the Buddhist practice of *metta,* or lovingkindness.[14]

* * *

The ultimate goal of dharma practice is to end individual and collective suffering, and to help us find freedom and joy through understanding and transforming the causes of our suffering. Our communities are vibrant only when we engage and ignite compassion within them to tear down the imbalances that cause harm and rebuild systems that honor the dignity and worth of all. By leading the charge from within our spiritual communities, channeling compassion into real change, we can finally, truly begin to belong to each other in this beautifully diverse world.

* * *

We can adapt the reflection Pádraig Ó Tuama offered to the L'Arche community into questions to ask ourselves and each other within our communities:

What do we really need to keep?
What are we afraid of losing?
What needs to grow in us?
What are we willing to let go of?
Are we willing to have our heart broken to let in the light?

chapter 5

transforming tension into possibility

*In general we must not wish for the disappearance of
any of our troubles, but grace to transform them.*

—SIMONE WEIL, *GRAVITY AND GRACE*

We All Need Help Finding Our Way

Vibrant communities practice holding tension between people in generative ways, enabling them to learn skills that can transform conflict into greater understanding. Most of us are not taught to do this; as a result, differences in points of view are often experienced as a problem to be avoided, confronted, or solved. These skills are very teachable and, when practiced, help us transcend an unfortunate mindset where someone's view is better or right.

Communities typically favor one of two approaches to hold their vision and handle their differences. Antiracism facilitator Donna Bivens describes these styles as *inquiry* and *conflict*. She notes that groups usually stick to one style rather than flexibly moving between them. Flexibility is important, though, to benefit from the strengths of each style while navigating their pitfalls.

Firmly rooted in a social justice orientation, Donna understands that conflict is at times necessary: "You can't get to what is happening if you don't honor the conflict." In her experience, people who stand primarily in inquiry tend to err toward conflict avoidance. On the other side, she observes, people who tend to gravitate toward conflict tend to remain there.

Donna explains that this polarizing habit of relying primarily on inquiry and avoiding conflict or—alternately, diving right into the fire—runs deep in all of us. To break the habit, we must cultivate awareness, acknowledging our personal tendency to tip to one side or the other. Reflection (which is part of inquiry) is necessary to move through conflict skillfully, but only when we are also willing and able to face conflict. And facing conflict then requires the skill of making room for it without tipping over into reactivity. In a time of great struggle like the one we are now in, it is critical to learn how to hold the tension between inquiry and conflict.

"After George Floyd, I thought, 'Okay, as long as you are in the tension between conflict and inquiry, you are doing it,'" Donna reflected. "On the other side of conflict is annihilation. Some people don't care about you. . . . At that point you are not in tension anymore. On the other side of inquiry is despair, that place where you feel you can't do anything."

How do we learn to be more reflective while at the same time having difficult conversations and taking necessary action? Donna finds the framework of the "tragic gap" helpful, which she learned about when she trained as a facilitator at the Center for Courage and Renewal, a center you will be introduced to later in this chapter.

Parker Palmer, who founded the Center for Courage and Renewal, coined the term *tragic gap* to refer to the place to stand that enables new possibility and keeps us out of the dangerous traps of toxic cynicism or irrelevant idealism. Toxic cynicism is a general belief that people aren't to be trusted, so the solution is to play the game, and ethics be damned. Irrelevant idealism is also a disempowered stance, one in which the state of feeling disillusioned or helpless leads to an unwillingness to engage. Palmer noted that these traps "sound like polar opposites but they take us to the same place, which is out of the action."

We can learn the skills of reflection, holding tension, and facing conflict when it is there without tipping over into reactivity. But these skills need to be practiced so we can begin to experience our differences as not always conflictual, and our conflicts as not always insurmountable. And the best training ground to practice these skills is within our existing communities.

● ● ●

Facilitators are sometimes needed to hold the space where people can navigate tension and practice healthy ways of relating. Facilitators teach the skills of cooperative and inclusive communication. These skills include patient and nonjudgmental listening, pausing, reflecting, and nonreactive responding.

Facilitators serve different functions for a community depending on the goals of the group. Communities sometimes want help articulating their mission statement to guide future planning and convey what they wish to create in the world. Or they have a clear purpose, and facilitators then help them move it forward such that everyone participates in generating clear, concrete goals. Sometimes communities with similar missions use facilitators so they can join forces to work toward an even larger vision.

When there is unhealthy conflict that is causing disruption and can't be successfully addressed within a community, facilitators can help. When different communities have a long history of conflict between them, support is needed to build trust and find common ground (an example of this will be introduced later in the chapter). And some communities come to a point where they choose to move on from each other; if that is the case, facilitation can help to disband with intentionality and integrity.

Whatever the goals, a facilitator creates an atmosphere of trust, connection, and cooperation over competition. Sometimes issues can't be readily resolved, yet it is still possible to better understand other points of view and find next steps to take.

The facilitator, who guides dialogue without directing it, is not responsible for making change happen. The underlying belief is that there is wisdom in the group, and kernels of change are cultivated under optimal conditions. Facilitated spaces encourage better listening, not only to other members but also to oneself. Here, people talk directly and authentically and can share their views without interruption. The goal is to create a safe space for participants to be vulnerable and, when necessary, say difficult things in an atmosphere of acceptance.

Trust is built during dialogue when people have the skills to meaningfully talk about their differences and, when possible, appreciate them. Without guidance and support, difficult conversations are often avoided in order to keep the peace, preserve relationships, or avoid judgment.

Although they can be challenging to navigate, these conversations can be had in ways that nourish and deepen relationships. Tension is natural, and conflict is sometimes an important part of the process that should not be avoided. But conflict is not the inevitable result of tension, nor are conflict and tension inevitably obstructions to finding solutions. When a group learns the skills to hold tension comfortably and confidently, it can unlock creative solutions that come directly out of their differences.

"The Heart behind the Words"

For eleven years beginning in 1974, Parker Palmer lived with his wife and children at Pendle Hill, a Philadelphia-area intentional community rooted in the Quaker tradition. Unlike many other faith-based communities, Pendle Hill attracted a diverse group of people from different lifestyles, backgrounds, and beliefs. Parker attributes this to the Quakers' style of worship, which encourages authenticity and includes practices to help people creatively hold their differences. While living in this community, he learned new ways to live in relationship, and he came to understand the profound power of silence.

"There's a famous story about Quaker and Native elders meeting in circles. An outsider observed, 'You speak two different languages; how did you communicate?' The Quaker said, 'We both know how to listen to the heart behind the words.'"

At Pendle Hill, Parker began to get answers to questions about community building he had long held—questions unanswered while earning his PhD in sociology, or later while community organizing in Washington, DC. When he was a graduate student at UC Berkeley, Parker saw community leaders hold on to control, a style of leadership that disempowered others within the community. Even when the power hierarchy didn't lead to exploitation, these communities grossly underused the capacities of their members.

During his work in DC, he learned a lot about conflict—how to hold it creatively and not run away from it. "We need a lot of creative conflict holding in this society," he said. But in these spaces, he didn't see that there were also opportunities for the kind of reflection that led to personal growth within the community.

The idea for the Center for Courage and Renewal (CCR) was to take a community like Pendle Hill on the road. Not everyone finds the intentional community lifestyle accessible or desirable, so Parker wanted to create a method that would help strengthen communities by expanding the capacity of the people within them to access and express their deepest humanity.

The intention behind CCR was to create temporary communities in which facilitators teach skills that enable retreat attendees to build community while connecting with themselves more deeply. The CCR facilitators set general boundaries, and within them people are encouraged to bring their whole selves—all their identities.

In 1997 the Fetzer Institute heard of the work Parker was doing, and they asked him if he would be interested in building these kinds of communities for teachers, to help them rekindle a passion for teaching. The institute's mission is to transform communities and societies into more loving ones by supporting the development and implementation of programs in areas such as faith and spirituality, democracy, education, and organizational culture. In this context, CCR came to life.

Parker had clarity that he did not want to create typical weekend community-building retreats. "I've been to a million of them where everybody climbs to the mountaintop and has great vision; by Monday they are back home, working and walking in the valley of death."

He wanted to find twenty-five people interested in a more substantial commitment: eight long-weekend retreats over the course of two years. They would participate in communities with nonhierarchical leadership, similar to the kind of leadership that creates conditions for effective teaching. Skilled facilitators run retreats at CCR using a proven method called the Circles of Trust. This method has a minimalist agenda, using only general principles and practices to create safe spaces and promote learning.

Within this general framework people have free rein for self-exploration and the opportunity to practice skills that create trusting relationships.

Members learn to be more present, witnessing and listening deeply, not only to one another but also to themselves. "People often say amazing things without knowing it," observes Parker. We don't often pause to reflect on our own important insights, giving them the consideration they deserve. By practicing the skills learned in the circle, members recognize their own truths, which has powerful consequences for their own lives and their communities.

Parker believes that a small community with relational skills, even one of limited duration, can have a deeper impact than a larger, ongoing community shaped by cultural norms. His insight speaks to the reality that there can be different paths of showing up for community that will help us build momentum for a more connected world. We long to belong, and the skills for creating healthy community are teachable; now is the time to bring our full-on commitment and vision to creating them.

● ● ●

John Fenner, the director of facilitator preparation at CCR, has been leading retreats there for over twenty years. He says the belief that everyone gets along well in community is a myth (and nostalgia for a time that never existed). "Community is really grist for our own personal work, the place where all our buttons get pushed. We increase the capacity to be in community by shaping how we get along with each other and handle conflict."

I spoke to John about the relationship skills learned within the Circles of Trust. He stressed that unlike some other groups focused on personal growth, participation within them is invitational, meaning members only share what they want to share about themselves. However, everyone is asked to learn and practice listening skills in relation to those in the group who choose to share.

Within the Circles of Trust there are touchstones, or principles, for how to be together and relate to other community members. One touchstone is deep listening—practicing attentive presence to support the person sharing. Many who participate in these circles discover, to their surprise, that deep listening does not come easily or naturally.

CCR once worked with nonprofit leaders and tested their listening skills before and after a five-retreat series held over six months. Interestingly, everyone in the group rated their listening skills lower the second time around! It's not that they listened with less skill the second time; to the contrary, they now more clearly recognized their challenges in listening. They had to learn not just to respond, which is the norm in most conversations, but also to pause more and try to really understand what the other person is saying.

Another important touchstone: there is no fixing, advising, or correcting each other. This practice eliminates much of our typical conversational content. When someone is grappling, or simply shares their challenges, feelings, or struggles, we often automatically rush into helping mode rather than creating space around what they're telling us.

Counterintuitively, this impulse to help is unhelpful because the person who gives advice has stopped listening. The person who had shared of themselves does not get to their own deeper truth. (Rule of thumb for unsolicited advice: pause once, twice, three times before offering. And still generally choose to listen more.) It is most helpful to listen with an attentive presence to what the other person shares, honoring it with space so that it can be digested and reflected upon.

A third touchstone is asking open and honest questions. These are not intended to satisfy the asker's curiosity, nor to guide the conversation in a predetermined way. They are the kinds of questions that help the person go deeper within, encouraging their own insights. These are questions such as, "Have you had an experience like this before?" or "What, if anything, would help you in this moment?" This one skill—asking open, honest, and relevant questions—unlocks more wisdom and creates space for a greater range of possibilities than in most attempts at problem-solving.

Deep listening, in combination with asking open and honest questions, creates a trusting atmosphere. The person speaking feels safe and is encouraged to tap into and trust their own wisdom.

Those listening and witnessing also benefit because they stretch themselves while they practice the skills of stillness, inquiry, and attentive presence. By listening in new ways to people's stories, compassion is kindled and deepened, as is the capacity to better know oneself. This work supports the individual's integrity while simultaneously building a community of authentic individuals who share their unique gifts with each other.

● ● ●

Since its beginnings, CCR has trained over three hundred facilitators who now work around the world. Circle of Trust retreats are attended by a diverse group of individuals, including those in the helping professions and leadership positions. Participants grow personally during the retreat and then return home to offer leadership, including leading retreats, in their own communities.

For example, the CEO of an accrediting organization for medical residency programs heard about CCR's initiative for K–12 teachers. It inspired him to do something for medical residency program directors who work in isolating conditions, leading to high burnout rates. He understood that helping those responsible for educating future doctors enriches their training programs and therefore medicine as a whole.

Out of his efforts, ten medical residency program directors from around the country participated in a Circles of Trust retreat. One of the attendees, Richard Shugerman, found what he learned in the retreat to be so incredibly helpful for his own growth that he wanted to provide the same opportunity for others.

Richard now leads a yearly retreat for program directors who have won a teaching award from the accrediting organization. Nearly everyone offered a spot in the annual retreat accepts. They come from all over the country and work within many disciplines of medicine. He believes that when the directors take these relational skills back to their programs, medical students benefit, becoming more empowered and thus better physicians. Next, Richard wants to offer this opportunity to all interested program directors, not only to the recipients of an award.

Richard finds that of all the touchstones, the skill of asking open and honest questions has had the greatest impact. Being told what to do every day shapes residents in unhelpful ways, making them less personally invested in their training programs. If program directors create a safe environment where they ask their trainees these kinds of questions, the doctors in training will develop the tools to answer their own questions and better understand themselves. This is a paradigmatic shift that flattens the hierarchy in medical training programs. In the new paradigm, trainees shape their own programs and invest more in their patients. And more collaborative medical training models will hopefully encourage better working partnerships between doctors and their patients.

• • •

I asked John Fenner about whether the Circles of Trust had ever been used with participants from groups with a long history of mistrust between them. He told me about the use of circles for dialogue between groups of Native and non-Native residents that took place on rural reservation land in Wagner, South Dakota. At the time, John was involved with a different kind of circle work with another organization. It was in this context that he met and befriended participants Vince Two Eagles and Amy Doom, who later facilitated future circles in the Wagner community. John introduced us, and because of the trust between the three of them, Vince and Amy were open to sharing their stories.

Using Circles to Talk about Race

The town of Wagner is a bicultural rural community of 1,600 people located within the exterior boundaries of the Yankton Sioux Tribe. The Dakota Nation is one of seven Sioux tribes that make up a confederation referred to as the Seven Council Fires. Their Indigenous name is *Ihanktonwan Dakota Oyate,* which means "people who camp at the end."

Native and non-Native communities are segregated in Wagner, and there is a long history of mistrust between them. The toxic national political discourse has infiltrated here, adding to existing tensions. The conflict between Native and non-Native people in South Dakota cannot be understood outside a historical context of injustice, trauma, and dominance. My understanding of the history in this area comes from Vince Two Eagles, a respected Dakota elder. (For further information on this history, Vince recommends the book *Pagans in the Promised Land: Decoding the Doctrine of Christian Discovery* by Steven Newcomb).

Conflicts between groups of people cannot be resolved without some agreed-upon understanding of how the conflict arose in the first place, says Vince. For too long the historical narrative reflected only the perspective of the dominant group. For any kind of progress, there needs to be a willingness to examine different perspectives on the source of the conflict that is present today.

One source of conflict in Wagner stems from the fact that the Yankton Sioux reservation is heavily "checkerboarded." This means that in the 1880s, under pressure from the east for greater western expansion, the federal government broke up tribal lands and opened them up to white settlers. A small plot of land was allotted to each tribal member, and the "leftover" tribal land was available for homesteading. Vince says that for the Native people who were impacted, checkerboarding is a source of ongoing injustice.

● ● ●

Amy Doom, a cofacilitator of the circle dialogues on racism, explained the history of how they came about. In 2008, Wagner was one of forty-two rural communities in South Dakota that received a small grant to explore the roots of poverty in their area. They used the seed money to conduct a series of conversations that took place within five groups, each made up of twelve participants. Out of these initial discussions surfaced a quiet, courageous voice that desired to explore a multicultural identity in Wagner.

After these initial conversations, some participants in the initial discussions wanted to go further. Racism wasn't talked about; the word itself was contentious, and there was discomfort calling it that. They initially tried to couch the word *racism* in other terms, but whether they used the word or not, it still felt the same, so they ended up calling their next effort racism study circles.

They sought and received a much larger grant to conduct these circles over the course of several years. The primary goal of this initiative was to develop a process that would enable trust building between these groups so they could continue the conversation and deepen their impact. The circles would occur under the umbrella of Horizons Project (now called East River Horizons), an organization that works with local communities.

Creating an envelope to safely hold differences between two communities with a long history of conflict is no small undertaking. Skilled facilitation is required to find common ground, which is the condition for all mutual understanding and change.

An organization called Everyday Democracy provided the communities with a structured format, in the form of a study guide, to talk about racism. John Fenner, with the Center for Courage and Renewal, and Al

Nygard, affiliated with North Dakota's Sitting Bull College near Standing Rock Reservation, were the ones from Everyday Democracy who trained the original facilitator group in Wagner.

Everyday Democracy's facilitators trained Vince Two Eagles and Amy Doom, both active and respected in their communities, in how to facilitate the circles on racism. Vince, who had been active in the American Indian Movement, is a musician and songwriter who has worked as a substance abuse counselor, and Amy was a health care provider and coordinator who had an established relationship with both the Native and non-Native communities.

As John came to know Amy and Vince during this time, he told them about the Circles of Trust retreats and wondered if they were interested in participating. The idea appealed to them. They traveled to Minneapolis to attend one "with all these high-end, burnt-out professionals who needed renewal," Amy said with humor.

● ● ●

After they were trained in facilitating the circles of racism, Amy and Vince worked as a team to lead the process. The format was a series of structured discussions in small groups, with each group composed of half Native participants and half non-Native participants. These circles explored racism's impact in their everyday lives. Participants identified strengths within both communities and then brainstormed action steps that might promote understanding between these groups in the larger Wagner community.

Each circle had six sessions, with the first two focused on trust and relationship building; the next two were educational, with participants reviewing data together; and in the last two sessions they chose actions that arose directly from the educational component. For example, the group examined the underrepresentation of Native leadership in the school district, where nearly half the students were Indigenous. Out of these discussions, the group designed actions to facilitate the inclusion of a broader range of voices in the process of electing school board members.

After several study circles, Amy and Vince realized that although there was important discussion about existing problems, they were not getting to the heart of the issues. They wanted to dive deeper in order to experience the healing potential of circles. They thought of their experience within the Circles of Trust, and the idea came to them to introduce this process into the study circles on racism. Because they weren't trained to facilitate in this way, they needed outside help. They used some of their grant money to make this happen. John Fenner returned for the Circles of Trust retreat, along with a Native American facilitator from Montana and an African American woman from Michigan to cofacilitate.

Using the relational skills learned in the Circles of Trust retreat, the study circles on racism could now hold a safer space to talk more candidly about racism. Participants were able to drill down into the question of what trust looks like. The skills the group learned and practiced within the Circles of Trust helped deepen the conversations and build trust, moving their process forward.

* * *

Out of the study circles on racism, community members developed an understanding and a method for how to best effect change. After a series of these circles, the members then looked back at all the action steps that were implemented from the study circles and rated them in terms of effectiveness. What they found was that taking small actions over time had the best traction.

Amy reflected on how they initially had these conversations with few financial resources to help them. She wondered whether, if they had gotten the large grant in the beginning, they would have chased a big goal that would have caused them to miss the crucial insight that small, persistent actions work best. Throwing resources at a problem isn't effective without the essential, sometimes slow, ongoing work of relationship building.

Amy is speaking to an important truth that larger change is initiated within grassroots communities where action is taken within the context of valued relationships. Outside help and resources are sometimes necessary, whether in the form of financial resources, facilitators, outside experts, or even governments (through effective policy), but they are not the impetus for transformative change.

"When you bring different people to the table to discuss things like resource allocation, everyone comes with their own agenda," Vince Two Eagles said. "The process is messy and must include everyone's opinion. Here, facilitative leadership is the kind of leadership that doesn't try to impose its views on how communities ought to develop. They help shape the dialogue process in a nonmanipulative way, to facilitate solutions that come out of the discussions.

"The healing work of reconciliation is complex," said Vince, "and sometimes there are real issues that we just cannot move beyond. In our organization we don't ignore the negative. But we focus on creating partnerships for change. That is more interesting. For example, there is a large problem with substandard housing for Indians here in Wagner. We are trying to guide a discussion that moves toward conciliation, looking for processes toward solutions. This is more helpful than finger pointing and blaming. If we retreat to cynicism and total mistrust as default positions, this will continue as a disease in our community."

Vince is referring to a process within Horizons where they are working to build coalitions to address the issue of substandard housing on the reservation and rural South Dakota in general.

"There are two ways you can move with any problem, however complicated it is: you can have a conversation, or you can have conflict," said Vince. "Most people would rather have a conversation to resolve problems, but they don't have the tools. What we have learned in the study circles on racism, we try to offer to others by helping them develop their own tools."

In the process of finding common ground and building trust, being sensitive to language is so important because words mean different things to different people, and the choice of a word can strike a nerve. Amy gives the example of a new lexicon that is slowly emerging in parts of Wagner, which came out of persistent dialogue across differences. This lexicon is bicultural and hybrid. It does not overlook or whitewash the reality of their history, but it still recognizes Wagner as a place that is now shared by Native and non-Native people. Vince believes it is important that this hybrid lexicon be secular in nature for the process of continuing to talk about shared values and common ground. But he also points out that using a common secular language for process leaves space to talk about different content, including spiritual traditions such as Native ceremonies and Christianity, that are culturally important to people's value systems.

● ● ●

Over the course of five years, there were fifteen study circles on racism in Wagner. They provided the foundation for the work that continues at Horizons: reducing racism by promoting understanding. When people from different groups encounter each other and share their stories, they don't want the other to suffer. Those who have been touched by the circles continue to work within a bicultural leadership model, taking small steps toward change.

Bonds as Strong as Blood

Vince's mother, Margaret Zephier, also participated in the study circles on racism. Margaret is a respected Dakota elder who, along with her father and brother, brought back the Sun Dance tradition to the Yankton Sioux Reservation (and the Dakota people). Before then—and in spite of the First Amendment right of freedom of religion—Native sacred ceremonies were banned in the early 1800s when the federal government promoted Christian education among Native Americans.[1] When this discriminatory legislation was finally repealed in 1978 under the American Indian Religious Freedom Act, Margaret envisioned the Sun Dance as a way to give her and her children a better life.

When Amy first arrived in South Dakota as a young public health nurse, fifteen years before she participated in the circles on racism, she met Margaret when visiting her home in this capacity. The women were drawn to each other, and Margaret became a kind of mentor to Amy. Their relationship grew over time, and eventually Margaret extended an invitation for Amy to become a relative through a sacred ceremony called *Hunka*.

Hunka is one of the Sioux people's seven sacred ceremonies, and the term translates into something like "the making of relatives." When someone has lost a child, after a mourning period they can adopt someone through *Hunka*. Years earlier, Margaret had lost her own daughter, who was close in age to Amy. The *Hunka* bond is considered inviolable, as strong as blood.

In the *Hunka* ceremony, gifts are offered to guests, a form of hospitality that expresses gratitude and creates right relationship. For an entire year, the two women saved up to give these gifts. During that same time period, Amy studied relevant Dakota teachings, attended sweat lodges, and prayed with the Turtle Society, a Native women's society founded by Margaret. The year of preparation leading up to the *Hunka* was a deepening of Amy's encounter with the Dakota culture. During the *Hunka* ceremony, both extended families shared a celebratory meal, during which Amy wore a traditional ribbon dress.

The sibling bond that Amy and Margaret forged in the *Hunka* created a deep level of trust between Amy and Vince, who are now considered siblings through the *Hunka*. This has served them well during difficult times within the circles or when dealing with tension between their respective communities.

"We are brother and sister now, and the whole tribe honors that," Vince said. "Our being family through the *Hunka* strengthened our communities. We are better able to hold tension. We are brother and sister in the real sense. Amy serves as a diplomat for those in the white community, and I do the same for the Indian community. We both have our fingers on the pulse."

● ● ●

Finding a Native voice to write a weekly opinion piece in the local newspaper, the *Wagner Post,* was the first action step that came out of the study circles on racism. The idea of a weekly column that offered a Native perspective, creating meaningful conversation between the two communities, fit well with the long-term goal of conciliation. Vince stepped up and offered to write the column, and he named it "The Rez of the Story." The column later became syndicated and ran in other papers reaching a wider audience, including the *Lakota Times.*

Vince used the column to educate non-Natives about some of the stereotypes held about Dakota people. He also used the opportunity to respond to articles in local papers that described Native people in disparaging ways, a not-uncommon occurrence. Vince says it is often couched in subtle ways, but the message is always some form of describing the Native community as basically dysfunctional, with the implication that the non-Native community is not.

Amy shared a powerful story of an event that occurred as a result of Vince's column. During the course of the column's five-year run, a group of Mennonites read it and then contacted Vince with a request to participate in a circle with Yankton Sioux tribe members. Eventually they arranged to meet. On the day of the circle about ten Mennonites, including a few elders, pulled up in a large van.

Toward the end of the circle, an elder Mennonite farmer spoke up. Social justice is a core value in the Mennonite faith tradition, and this man had a strong desire to take ownership of the way his people had acquired their land. He said, "I want to make this right."

Amy continued the story: "Margaret was . . . in this circle and spoke to the farmer: 'I was sitting in my sewing room thinking about tonight. Thinking about why you have come here.' And what she said next was the straw that broke the camel's back: 'I thought to myself, has anybody welcomed you to this land?'"

"After Margaret said that, there was silence," remembered Amy. "We now understood the direction forward. Everything in the circle ripened us for this moment."

As Amy finished the story, the image of Margaret welcoming this man gave me chills, and the word *grace* came to mind.

The dominant culture continues to pay a high psychic price for its history, imposing even higher costs on those who have already suffered from past ignorance and wrongdoing. At that moment in the circle, Margaret's compassion showed how redemption works, which begins with the sincere intention to make things right, and the offer of mercy.

If we wish to fully belong to humanity, we must work for the kind of change that represents a fundamental paradigmatic shift. There is no other way. For example, the existing commitments made to Native peoples through treaties must be honored. Only when we learn to listen—in some ways for the first time—can there be conciliation and healing. Then we can begin to learn to live in peace with each other.

Vibrations Travel to the Present

There have been no formal study circles in Wagner for a few years, yet the dialogue continues within small groups and within the tragic gap— the space between what is possible and what exists in reality. What exists, oftentimes, is intolerable race relations. "What is ultimately possible is currently unattainable," said Amy. "You start with the tension in the middle, where social change takes place, or you stay home."

Amy said they persist "because for a long time this was the only space where dialogue happened. That is valuable. To stop is to suffocate. When we have bicultural dialogue, there is life-giving breath to the corpse that we once were. We don't want to go back to that place."

According to Amy, having had so many study circles over the course of five years created a kind of vibration that continues today. Past actions had a ripple effect and are felt in today's efforts to create multicultural relationships. For example, one of the early action steps was to create a community garden space. What came out of the community garden was the idea for a farmers' market. Then the farmers' market inspired them to ask the question, "How do we help people in generational poverty get access to fresh fruits and vegetables?"

The East River Horizons team continues its mission of promoting multicultural relationships, inviting any interested resident and organization to participate, and offering access to their facilitators. Horizon's bicultural leadership continues to meet regularly, using the skills first learned in the Circles of Trust. Horizon leaders now include young people who weren't participants in the study circles on racism. People "are touching the dialogue and receiving its effects," said Amy, including those not on Horizon's leadership team. "Most importantly, the dialogue never stops."

• • •

Both Vince and Amy insist on sharing the success stories. It can be easy to focus only on the suffering that exists within the community, which is the result of poverty, trauma, and continued segregation. For those who care, and who care to look, there are many signs of positive change.

Stories from within the circles were retold outside them, touching those who did not participate. For example, a story of conciliation loosely based upon the time when Margaret welcomed the Mennonite farmer became a children's book titled *The Medicine Quilt.*[2] Vince's mother Margaret created the Turtle Society for young Indigenous women, which offers sweat lodges and other traditional ways of healing. When the action steps were later evaluated for their effectiveness, Margaret's Turtle Society was considered the most impactful. And in 2021, after a hiatus, Vince once again started to write installments of "The Rez of the Story," offering balanced and compassionate wisdom to readers of the *Lakota Times*.

There are now opportunities in Wagner for Native and non-Native people to interact in social situations that weren't possible before. Spending time together and working toward a common goal are important steps to overcoming fear and igniting compassion.

The First Annual Unity Jam at Wagner Lake Park was organized by Horizon's leadership. The celebration honored the Boys and Girls Club youth of the year. Dance and music performances spanned the cultural spectrum of Wagner: Czech dance and German gospel music, and traditional Native dance and music.

In an effort to promote cross-fertilization of ideas, Horizons brought in outside consultants to lead workshops on topics relevant to the greater Wagner community. For example, Dr. Donna Beegle gave a workshop on the culture of poverty, offering ideas for how to shift from stereotypes and judgment to a deeper understanding of the causes of poverty. She herself had been chronically homeless before earning her doctorate, and now she works toward creating better models to lift people out of poverty. And Juana Bordas, award-winning author of *Salsa, Soul, and Spirit: Leadership for a Multicultural Age* and *The Power of Latino Leadership: Culture, Inclusion, and Contribution* led a workshop in which she offered wisdom from her experiences with diversity, leadership, and organizational change.

• • •

Vince can't yet say how the impact of the study circles on racism translates within the larger Wagner community, but he is cautiously optimistic: "Reconciliation is a long-term goal. We removed the prefix *re-* and called it *conciliation*. You can't be reconciled if you've never been conciled. As we defined it, conciliation is that ideal that has to do with justice and peace and those kinds of things that we all want. You can look at it like there's a door there to go through. There are barriers, and of course, racism is one of them. After several years of study circles, we were able to get to the point where we were willing to go through that door, together, to face the unknown. With intentionality, we resolved enough of the differences in our history so that we had the tools needed to go through that door, and to begin to look at 'what does conciliation look like?'"

Change happens regardless of how we feel about it, Vince said. He hopes that the balance tips and more people in Wagner believe that change can be directed for the good of everyone. For those working toward it, it moves at a pace that is often hard to recognize as progress. But we must stay at it, and if Vince can see possibility and persist given the history that he and his people have endured, then every one of us can.

"To move forward, we must keep commitments that we make within the dialogue," Vince said. In the circle, the name of the game is connection and integrity through relationships. When there is integrity and connection, the circle holds the wisdom for creative solutions, resilience, and the possibility of conciliation.

Although sometimes Vince is discouraged, he continues to take the long view: "If we are to have any kind of future, we must believe that the human spirit can transcend culture, color, and language. If we can manage that, then we will be okay." Vince's words brought to mind Amy's deep, personal conviction. She told me, "Here's the deal. If someone is going to save this country from falling off a cliff, on so many levels, not only environmentally but in how we treat each other, it's the Native people who have been treated so horribly."

ritual connects us to each other while pointing beyond

The way that can be spoken of
Is not the constant way;
The name that can be named
Is not the constant name.

                —LAO TZU, *TAO TE CHING*

A Latina Folk Herbalist Takes Cues from Plants

One of Jennifer Rose Marie Serna's earliest memories is of making potions in the tub following a visit to her great-grandmother. Jennifer's "Granny" was a *yerbatera*—someone who has an intimate knowledge of plants. Jennifer loved to watch Granny interact with her plants. "She'd walk past them and knew when they were thirsty," she said. "Or, 'you are telling me to harvest you now?'"

The whole family had affection for Granny's old ways, but it was Jennifer who felt a deep connection to them. "Granny would have been a *curandera* [a traditional healer] if life hadn't been so difficult for her," she explained. Granny had come over the border into the US at age seven with extended family who treated her as their servant. She awoke every morning before sunrise to feed everyone, and at one point they placed her in an orphanage. "Her native healing skills had to be used for survival," Jennifer said. Although Granny didn't have the title of *curandera,* she was a true plant person to whom her community came for healing.

Though raised more Latina than Indigenous, Jennifer always connected with this other side of her lineage. As a teenager she consciously began the journey toward reclaiming her Indigenous soul, which above all else is about connecting to what is wild. Jennifer learned ways to honor the land and the people living in close connection to it, and the unseen that is present in everything alive. She uses the word *unseen* as others might use *spirit* or *consciousness*—words that represent the source of all things. Jennifer's language intentionally reflects a less individualistic mindset and a more direct relationship with the natural world. Reclaiming her Indigenous spirit, or soul, ultimately means living as a human who does not enslave other beings.

Jennifer moved with her family at age five from Los Angeles to the Oregon coast. When she was in high school, her family felt excitement and pride when she received a full scholarship to the Oregon university of her choice. She arrived on campus and within one day knew that this kind of learning, primarily through books, was not for her. Without having words for it at the time, she intuited that she needed a more connected, experiential approach. Jennifer left school, got married, and became a mother. The maternal experience deepened her commitment to heal her family naturally with plants and herbs. For example, of her four children who are now teenagers and young adults, only one has ever been on antibiotics.

Learning what it means to live in harmony with the natural world has been emotionally heavy at times. Jennifer grieved for lost access to Indigenous ways, and she had to do a lot of investigating on her own. "That's really what being in this time and space is here in the US," she said. Reflecting on her experience of being a young mother, she had to learn Native ways without the guidance of elders. Yet she is grateful for her close-knit and supportive family, her parents who helped raise her children, and her Granny who was also an important presence.

She prayed to her ancestors and listened for their guidance. Along the way, she developed important friendships with other women on a similar path of reclaiming their lineages and rituals. They supported each other's efforts to uncover lost traditions and integrate them back into their lives. Together they prayed to their ancestors, filling the gaps in their knowledge and sharing what they learned with family and each other.

Jennifer credits her teacher, Martín Prechtel, for growing her understanding of how to begin to cultivate food differently. Prechtel, who is half First Nations and half Swiss, uses storytelling, riddles, music, and ritual to help his students connect to the natural world and their ancestral culture. Jennifer's two years spent studying at his school in New Mexico, Bolad's Kitchen, fostered the ingenuity for becoming self-reliant in this modern world. For her this means that in addition to cultivating her own food and medicine, she can make her own clothes, weave rugs, fish, and even do a bit of plumbing, enough to have a real appreciation for the gifts and livelihoods of others.

● ● ●

After Jennifer's third child was born, her father wanted to live closer to his grandchildren. Three days later he found a thirty-two-acre parcel of land with a house on Sauvie Island, just ten miles from downtown Portland, Oregon. Here Jennifer and her extended family, including both sets of grandparents, lived in a communal way. It is on this land that Jennifer has been deepening her connection to the unseen.

Sauvie Island, with over twenty-four thousand acres, is one of the largest river islands in the United States. Situated between the Columbia and Willamette Rivers, it has been an epicenter of human habitation for thousands of years and was home to the Multnomah band of the Chinook Tribe. Within a few decades of the arrival of Europeans at the turn of the nineteenth century, nearly all the Indigenous peoples died from a malaria epidemic, and by the 1830s the island was uninhabited.[1] The Hudson Bay Company established large dairy farms on the island, and farmers settled there because of the fertile soil.

Half of Sauvie Island is a now a protected wildlife area, with the rest being used primarily for farming. It is known for bird-watching, beaches, and U-pick berry fields. Jennifer experiences the island as a portal that attracts people to it—and kicks people off of it. After she divorced, she wondered if she could stay there with her children and make ends meet. Farming on a small scale at the time, Jennifer made prayers to the land to help her. The land heard her, letting her stay and thrive. This was the beginning of Wapato Island Farm, a small community of three farmers and their families who live and work together to wildcraft herbal and mushroom medicines.

Jennifer, who practices folk traditions to cultivate food and plant medicine, works as a practitioner of ancestral healing. Her business partner, Rae Hart, is a fungi farmer, nurse, and bee tender. Lyndsey Trapp is a flower farmer and massage therapist who makes native and medicinal bouquets using the farm's bounty. Working hard, side by side, builds a deep sense of trust between the women within this small community.

The farm's apothecary is the manifestation of Jennifer's dream of a medicine house. The apothecary is where she, Rae, and Lyndsey craft medicine from ethically harvested plants grown on the farm or harvested in Oregon's wilderness. Nearly fifty herbs are grown there, including those abundant in the Pacific Northwest, such as milky oats and Oregon grape. Different kinds of plant medicine are made in conjunction with different cycles of the year. In the fall, they generally make medicines using mushrooms and the roots of plants; in winter they use buds, leaves, and bark; in spring they work with leaves and flowers; and in the summer they use leaves, flowers, and fruit.

Handcrafted offerings include tinctures to calm the nerves, syrup for lung support, smoked herbal bath salts, salve with skin-healing herbs, and immune-boosting elixirs. The farmers are committed to serving as health and healing resources to local communities who identify as Black, Indigenous, or people of color, offering plant medicine and workshops regardless of ability to pay.

The sacred Three Sisters crops of corn, beans, and squash are also grown on the farm. Jennifer will introduce hemp to the farm because it has many uses, such as a great base for soap, a source of vitamins E and A, and mold-resistant insulation. And hemp is kind to the earth: it uses little water, reduces erosion, and regenerates the soil.

Indigenous practices, though labor intensive, are preferred to modern farming methods because they are more respectful to the land. For example, Jennifer and her companions don't use tractors; they plant by gently opening up the soil with a broadfork, which keeps much of the mycelium network intact. They leave areas of the land less cultivated, and they work more with native plants rather than annual ones. Native species of plants require less water and attract pollinators. To honor the unseen, a two-acre tract of land remains wild without disruption from human activity, and the land has since become habitat for a greater variety of wild animals, including a beaver who now lives on the pond.

● ● ●

Rituals are an integral part of farming practices at Wapato Island Farm; they serve to honor and commemorate the plants, the ancestors, and the unseen. When it is time to harvest seeds, the farmers hold a ceremony to pay their respects. They collect seeds from the best-quality plants, which are then dried, processed, and stored for the spring. During the ceremony, the seeds are first laid out on the ground so they can be seen, appreciated, and thanked. Some corn might be popped and set on an altar to express gratitude to the ancestors for their guidance in transmitting this important practice.

Seed saving, a practice that has been in existence for twelve thousand years, is of central importance on the farm. Only in the latter part of the twentieth century did most farmers begin buying seeds from corporate suppliers, who then pushed to outlaw the ancient practice of seed saving. This transition has not served humans or the planet, because seed saving creates resilient plants by increasing biodiversity.

Bottling medicine is another example of a communal ritual. The task is celebratory and social, while also infused with a reverent quality. The farmers are joined by other communities, such as an urban Indigenous group, who arrive earlier in the day for conversation and a shared meal. When Jennifer and Rae are ready for help with bottling the medicine, women and girls join in the farm's event space, named Abuela Tecolate. Conversation and music permeate the large, open-air room as the bottles are filled. Any medicine that spills onto the tables does not go to waste. It is seen as auspicious to rub the spilled medicine on your body to receive its benefits.

Life is ritual for Jennifer, and she has nonformal, personal, and meaningful rituals that are an integral part of her daily life. Many of these include beautiful gratitude practices. For example, before eating she sets aside the first bite as an offering, sometimes placing it on her altar. She has tea at night and thanks the plants that made it. When her children were young, she had a ritual of reading to them every night. "What is more special than giving them my time, and a good story to inspire us, taking us to dream time?" she asked.

For Jennifer, ceremony and ritual are somewhat different from each other. Rituals are part of her everyday, personal world, and they may or may not include others. Ceremony is a ritual specifically shared with her community; it derives its power from the trust built between people. On the farm, that trust comes out of working together and showing up for each other in times of need. Because ceremony is, first and foremost, about relationship, it is deliberate and intentional. "You don't just show up in someone else's community and participate in their ceremonies," Jennifer said. It is about being present to each other, cocreating meaning and a future that reflects what the community most values.

Rituals are also an integral part of the folk healer's work. Jennifer uses plants and intention to create rituals in her consultations. She often starts with a cleansing practice called a *limpia*. For the rituals she chooses plants and herbs with calming properties and doesn't personally use them for their psychoactive properties. Jennifer also works with vibrations through drumming or breath. Informed by the guidance of plant spirits and ancestors, these healing rituals create an atmosphere of safety in which someone can release difficult or painful emotions. In Jennifer's view, what gives the ritual power is the act of someone reaching out for help and having a caring person on the other end who is available. The plants heal the body and mind. The rituals, performed within the context of a caring relationship, are also powerful medicine.

● ● ●

Wapato Island Farm is a place of convergence for several communities who share a commitment to honoring the earth and learning about its healing power. They form a tight-knit metacommunity, supporting each other and sharing ceremonies. For example, they practice seed saving together, which is part of all their lineages, though none of them were connected to the practice before they met. Now, together, they are learning this tradition that is crucial to preserving food culture.

One of these communities is 7 Waters Canoe Journey, an urban Indigenous group whose mission is to connect to their traditional canoe culture as a way of healing their families. They take annual canoe journeys where they use song, dance, and storytelling to return to the ways of their ancestors. On Wapato Island Farm they have a small plot of land where they grow food, and they spent a year carving a twenty-foot spruce dugout canoe that now has a home on the Columbia River.

These communities learn and reconstruct what they can about their ancestors, their traditions, and the origins of their ceremonies. These reclamation efforts are held as sacred. Rituals may occasionally be modified in ways that are meaningful in the present. Sometimes the journey is painful because knowledge has been lost. The knowledge they reclaim is passed on to their children, an important part of any tradition, but also to their elders because they, too, have lost access to the old ways.

Jennifer has a special connection to members of the Mayan migrant community who work on nearby farms. Over time, a friendship has developed between them. Working long hours for little compensation, this community has little time and means for participating in their cultural ceremonies. Jennifer engages her Instagram community to raise funds to supply the roughly thirty-five families with the basics to live. She also picks up meals from the Native American Youth and Family Center and delivers them to the families.

Carmen is a matriarch in this Mayan community; she and Jennifer are like family to each other. As neither is fluent in Spanish, which is their only shared language, the way they communicate and show care extends beyond words. The farmers raised money to build a *temescal,* a traditional Mayan sweat lodge, outdoors on the farm. And Jennifer created a small office within the event space for Carmen to practice traditional healing, tending to the mind, body, and spirit of the Mayan community.

These communities offer songs and blessings to each other. The Canoe Journey might sing a traditional song of women's empowerment to the Mayans. Carmen offers her prayers in return. They don't always understand the meaning of the blessing, but they comprehend the heart and energy behind the words.

Holding Experience and Making Meaning

In addition to elevating the mundane by finding meaning in it, rituals bring solace and strength in difficult times. They create a safe space for the full range of shared human experience—joy and pleasure as well as pain and grief. Watching a community's rituals tells us a lot about what they most value.

Every culture ritualizes certain life events, rites of passage such as births and graduations, commitments of love, and death. Transitional rituals honor where we have been, recognizing our growth and effort, while helping take us to what is next. Just as important are personal rituals that create a pause to honor life's moments.

We participate in rituals because they symbolically remind us of what we hold most dear, what we consider sacred, and connect us to it. A song becomes a ritual when it is sung to connect us to our traditions, as an act of devotion, or in celebration. Cooking a meal becomes a ritual when we prepare the food with loved ones in mind, with gratitude for the people, plants, and animals that made the meal possible, or when it is shared with others to make them feel like honored guests. Walking is a ritual when it is undertaken as a way to clear the mind, invite creativity, or be more present to the natural world.

As intentional, repetitive efforts, good habits have something in common with rituals, but they differ in an important way. The purpose of habit is to make the action more effortless, whereas ritual calls for deliberateness, priming the mind to heighten the experience. The beauty of ritual is that when it is enacted with intention, the process has a quality of elevated presence.

Finding pleasure in shared experience is important to a community. Collectively savoring the good things in life helps us move through its challenges with grace and resilience. Through celebration, as a kind of ritual, we experience and express gratitude for the abundance we have and for each other.

Rituals are ultimately about belonging—to ourselves, to community, to the natural world, to that which is greater than we are. By practicing the rituals we were raised with, creating new ones, or connecting to those of our ancestors, we enhance the experience of community and connection. Rituals become meaningful when practiced over time and with earnestness, which enables us to live in closer alignment with our values and beliefs.

* * *

The degree of disruption to our collective rituals caused by COVID-19 is incalculable, as is the resulting experience of loss. Couples cancelled or radically altered their wedding plans, and birthday celebrations were muted. First responders didn't go home to their families for months, making the difficult choice to keep them safe from infection.

We only connected with friends and extended support systems from a distance. Families missed holiday gatherings, and we no longer greeted each other with hugs and handshakes.

When the pandemic upended our rituals and celebrations, we became painfully aware of how important they are for our essential well-being. We thought a lot about what we most missed and how we'd gather when we could again safely meet. Virtual community was both a godsend and bittersweet as we experienced its possibilities and its limitations. Out of necessity, we found ways to adapt our rituals. Birthdays became drive-by events, and lawn signs celebrated recent graduates. The elbow bump replaced the hug and handshake, and extended families connected via Zoom. Nuclear families rediscovered rituals such as sitting down together for evening meals.

Perhaps nowhere was the disruption to communal gatherings felt more painfully than in end-of-life rituals, which help us grieve and move through loss. One of the most excruciating realities was that families couldn't be at their loved ones' sides when they died. There were no in-person wakes, funerals, or shivas, all rituals that honor who we've lost and support those who are left to grieve. The lack of physical togetherness, the inability to show up with a hug or just sit near the bereaved without saying a word, made the mourning process isolating and more difficult.

Ritual is one of the most powerful tools to heal the collective pain we hold because it is a way to connect us. In addition to the loss resulting from the pandemic itself, the extended pause imposed by long-term social distancing heightened our awareness of other kinds of loss. These losses had been there all along, but many of us had not consciously faced them. In 2020 we could no longer avoid the pain caused by our nation's deep divisions and our inability to communicate across our differences. Americans faced, perhaps in a way they never had, the grief entailed by acknowledging the legacy of our racist and oppressive structures.

We need rituals, shared and personal, to express our yearnings and our pain and to help us aspire to something larger than our personal concerns, as important as they are. Rituals connect us to our past, enabling us to own both its beauty and darkness, in order to point us to a different future.

● ● ●

The bonds within a community are deepened when its members create and practice rituals that reflect their core values and wholesome, heartfelt longings. Some rituals shaped us when we were young. These childhood rituals continue to resonate within our psyches, even when they no longer align with our beliefs or adult ways of making meaning. Within our communities we can hold conversations about our ancestors and their values as reflected in their rituals, not to put them on a pedestal or elevate the past above the present but to honor them.

Communities can cocreate rituals that acknowledge different traditions, together choosing what they want to honor and commemorate. Which rituals do members have in common? Are the beliefs behind them or the meaning they hold the same, or different? For example, do people have different rituals that honor similar things, such as sitting shiva or holding a wake, to get support from the community during a time of mourning? As rituals are repeated within our communities, they become touchstones that give an added sense of purpose to our shared lives.

In diverse communities there will be differences in what people find important to ritualize, as well as how to do it. It shouldn't be assumed that the rituals of the majority, such as Christmas in the United States, will be what the whole community celebrates. If Christmas is an important holiday, can Hanukkah, Kwanzaa, and winter solstice also be celebrated if they are meaningful for others in the community?

Within our communities we can be inclusive in how we approach rituals, being sensitive to every person's history with them. Some people have been marginalized by lack of access to the larger culture's rituals, such as when they experience loss in a way that isn't honored in their communities. For example, someone who is divorced may feel like a failure and may have difficulty processing the loss. A community ritual that symbolizes the importance of what that relationship had been, as well as the pain of its ending, can be tremendously healing. Or a couple who experienced a miscarriage may not have processed their grief fully because we don't often talk about that kind of loss, and it's treated as a medical event. A community ritual can honor the unborn child and the parents by recognizing the love and dreams that they held in their heart for their baby.

Cultural rituals of celebration also exclude some people. A good example of this is that until recently same-sex couples could not be legally married in the United States (and still cannot in much of the world). There are all kinds of committed relationships that would be meaningful to ritualize that aren't valued in the larger culture. In addition, people need to be celebrated for courageous acts of authenticity, such as claiming identities that the dominant culture judges harshly. For example, people who come out as nonbinary or trans can face cruelty when trying to live authentically, but instead such acts should be celebrated.

Community ritual can recognize and celebrate persistent efforts and hard work. We can do this, for example, by honoring a young adult who did not go to college yet who worked long and hard to find their vocation. They need for their accomplishment to be recognized as much as a college graduate needs a ceremony to mark a completed phase of life. These are just a few of the important life circumstances that vibrant communities can ritualize in creative ways.

A New York Theater Returns to Its Ancient Roots

As a teenager in California, Adam Greenfield discovered the work of playwrights. To a young person struggling to find where he fit in, these works became portals to alternate worldviews. Watching local theater gave him tools to process his experience and helped him access a wider range of emotions. Most importantly, plays made his life more interesting and mysterious. All Adam wanted was to land in New York City and be part of its vibrant theater culture.

Adam realized his dream in 2007, when he moved to New York to join the staff of Playwrights Horizons, a respected off-Broadway theater, as literary manager. He read plays for a living and later produced them. Playwrights Horizons is known for cultivating the next generation of artists as well as encouraging the new works of veterans. In its fifty-year history, this theater has nurtured the development of nearly four hundred American playwrights, lyricists, and composers.

In 2020 Adam took up the reins there in the role of artistic director, just as COVID-19 shuttered the season. The crisis created an extended pause for reflection and discussion around questions such as "How do we more deeply engage with communities in the city?" and "When the curtains rise again, how can theater return to its roots as a civic ritual?"

* * *

The pandemic exposed foundational cracks in the practice of making theater as an institution, contradictions that had been identified earlier but not addressed. On the one hand, plays were produced with more diverse themes than ever before, and by a greater diversity of writers. But the problem was: who was watching them? Theater, like all institutions, has significant issues of who has access and who is being represented in the plays. Can theater reinvent itself by returning to its roots, making plays that are relatable and available to everyone? Can it become more than a form of entertainment, even more than an art form, and provide the important civic function of engaging broader communities?

When Western theater first evolved in ancient Greece, Adam explained, it wasn't for the purpose of making money: "Tragedy emerged out of a recognition that there were injustices in the world, like 'why do good people suffer?' And the event that we now call theater filled a deep need for ritual, to reconcile great conflicts and questions, like Sophocles posed in *Antigone:* 'What happens when the needs of the individual are at odds with the needs of the state?'"

Theater in ancient Greece, at its essence, was a civic ritual deeply interwoven into the fabric of daily life. It was a kind of pop-up community where people could step back from the daily grind and participate in something greater than themselves.

In the United States, theater has distanced itself from its roots as civic ritual and evolved into a for-profit venture, which created barriers of access for many communities. In the 1970s, when Playwrights Horizons was founded, there was a push to professionalize and institutionalize theater. For example, many theaters adopted a business model of paid subscriptions, seeking money up front to allow for consistent program planning. Theaters became associated with their buildings, which sprang up in neighborhoods where residents were more likely to give money. "People went in search of the white dollar," Adam reflected. "And that sort of established . . . the theatergoing community, which is notoriously older, upper middle class, and white."

Before Playwrights Horizons joined the movement for institutional stability, it was a scrappy theater originally located in the West Village before moving to Queens, then relocating again to Hell's Kitchen in what was once an old burlesque hall. After Playwrights Horizons raised over $30 million, they had the old building knocked down and built a new one with terrazzo floors and glass walls. The company's new home debuted in 2002, and the transformation defined it as an institution for a particular audience.

＊ ＊ ＊

When theater doors closed due to COVID, many theatrical productions moved to digital formats like Zoom. Adam and his colleagues at Playwrights Horizons chose not to go this route. They believed theater has to be experienced in person for it to have its full impact.

Instead, they used the downtime for reflection and dialogue. Ashley Chang, a dramaturg, had the idea of creating a magazine, *Almanac,* as a way to expand upon these conversations.

Before the pandemic, many artists and playwrights were questioning the direction that theater had taken. The extended pause created space to envision how to return in a way that would be more inclusive of the communities that make New York the vibrant city it is. Could Playwrights Horizons maintain some stability while at the same time deinstitutionalizing the theater? Could they be more intentional in creating access, welcoming a wider audience to their productions?

Moving forward, Playwrights Horizons will test out new models for production, including getting out of its building in midtown Manhattan and performing in other neighborhoods. Adam hopes to create malleable, mobile productions to transport plays from its Hell's Kitchen location to venues throughout the city to reach underserved communities. Additionally, the company will produce plays less expensively so they can offer more affordable ticket prices. Outside funding will still be welcome and necessary, but more effort will go toward finding ways for New Yorkers of all stripes to experience the theater.

"It's not enough to lower ticket prices or even give them away," Adam said. "We actually want to bring our work to you and give it to you for free. We want to be community with you, and hopefully at some point you can find your way to us. So that, hopefully, we can share the city together."

• • •

Playwrights Horizons's first postpandemic production was a play titled *What to Send Up When It Goes Down,* written by Aleshea Harris. The entire play was conceived as a community ritual that bears witness to the physical and spiritual deaths of Black men and women who have died at the hands of police and others. The playwright intended the work to mirror the insane reality in which an unarmed Black person can be killed with no accountability. In the introductory note to the play, Harris explains that this is a real ritual, not a performative one: "We are sincerely gathered to honor those who have been taken too soon." She says that the play is first and foremost a ritual for Black people, though non-Black people are welcome if they show up with conscientious presence. The play is constructed as ritual space in hopes that it can offer a place for discussion, catharsis, and healing.

The ritual begins before the audience enters the theater space, as they wait in the lobby surrounded by blown-up photographs of the dead. Some of them will be widely recognized—Sandra Bland, Eric Garner, Tamir Rice—but most will not. As the audience members enter the theater space, the actors stand at the doorway and welcome people as they enter, making eye contact as they do.

During the first part of the performance, the audience stands in a large circle with the actors interspersed among them. The lines between audience and actors are blurred as each person is asked to be part of the conversation on racism, offering their feelings, thoughts, and hopes for the future. The emotion in the air during the interactive part, although contained by the newness of the experience, was palpable.

Then the audience takes their seats, and the actors perform a series of vignettes while in motion, the intense energy a container for the expression of rage and other emotions like joy, grief, and love. The ritual concludes differently depending on whether an audience member identifies as Black: toward the very end of the play the audience separates, with the Black audience members remaining in the performance space while the others move to the lobby, and all participants having an ending to the ritual before leaving the building.

The playwright ingeniously uses theater-as-ritual to distinguish groups, intentionally prioritizing one without excluding anyone, which creates a container for powerful, uncomfortable experiences. As a white audience member, I felt both part of what was happening and aware that the play was not for me, yet I wasn't an outside observer. When I left the theater, I wasn't sure how to process the experience, but I sensed that a seed was sown and would evolve. *What to Send Up When It Goes Down* functions as a powerful ritual in that it points to something beyond it. I personally was left with a sense of hope that if we could create experiences similar to what Harris had done with her work, then we can stand within the painful paradox of our separateness, while together confronting the racial violence that perpetuates it.

* * *

Although not all of the plays produced at Playwrights Horizons will be so explicitly ritualistic in content, greater accessibility in formatting will enable them all to function better as community ritual. For Adam Greenfield, choosing great plays is necessary but no longer enough. The most pressing challenge now is how to engage more of the people within the city. "It's going to take a lot of trial and error, and it's going to be a big effort. How do you get everyone into the big tent? We want to do theater for all. And we have to earn everyone's trust in order to build a space in which this can happen."

* * *

A primary function of both art and ritual is that they point to what lies beyond them. However, in our culture, entertainment is often the primary goal of theater. "You have to believe that both you and people making art are humbled by a larger purpose," explained Adam. "It's kind of like going to church or participating in some other community ritual in that way. I'm going to get less out of it sometimes than other times. I hope theater can help cultivate faith in the act of participation, as something larger, for everybody. You might go to a play and get nothing out of it. You might go to a play and it changes you. What I hope is that more people will participate.

"I think because of the speed of the culture we live in, audiences want to digest things quickly and move on. Audiences want to look at a story, understand what the theme is, and be able to spit it back. Plays have become products, like 'I'm buying this ticket and the play is going to deliver goods to me. And those goods need to be reliable and proven.' And so art has become commodified. But that is not how I believe art functions in a healthy culture."

Audiences may need help in viewing themselves as a member of the theater community rather than as a consumer of a product. Now when Adam produces a play, he thinks more about creating the atmosphere around it. When the audience walks into the performance, he wants them to understand that they are walking into a place of experimentation, a place of thought, of newness and freshness of ideas. "To get the full experience of what a play has to offer, you need to stop, slow down, and meet it on its level," he said. "The more you slow down, the more you pick up.

"Ultimately, I hope that the reason people keep coming to this theater is because they want to be infused with the mystery."

When a Sage Points to the Moon, a Fool Stares at the Finger

Ritual points to something that cannot be fully grasped. But people can be more attached to the ritual itself than to the mystery to which it points. When this happens, rituals become dogmatic and exclusive, and their participants miss the forest for the trees. Thomas Brackett, who trains Episcopalian church leadership worldwide, put it this way: "You know the ancient Chinese adage of the wise person pointing to the moon and the fool obsessed with the finger? We've become obsessed

with the finger, which is more accessible than the moon. A lot of ritual
has become an end in itself and we forgot why it was there."

When rituals are used to heighten a person or group's power, or to try
to elevate someone's prestige, they are misused and their real purpose is
lost. "We mess it up," explained Thomas. "There is the troublesome reality
of how we form power. Fewer and fewer of us have had local experiences
of meaning making. We are not creating spaces for the sacred to show
up. [We look to] expert stories told by an expert teller to be processed
in expert, intellectual ways. [This] leaves out the body and the feminine.
Leaves out the interstitial spaces between us."

For Thomas, the essence of the Christian tradition is about gathering community in ways that call up the creative presence of the divine
among us. That happens on the local level, where people meet in their
homes or around a fire pit. Institutional church as a hierarchical power
over the Christian community was not part of the original practices and
intent. "Jesus, the Palestinian rabbi, said, 'when two or three of you are
gathered in my name,'" Thomas explained. "He is pointing to something
that is accessible to us all."

Church as represented by local, personal gatherings is where the big
questions are explored, said Thomas. Within our gatherings we don't
have to have all the answers, but we hold the questions and learn to
be comfortable with uncertainty. "And if they are liberated souls not
beholden to any external agency, they explore together to figure out,
'What are those activities that remind us, with as few words as possible,
of who we are?'"

Thomas's understanding of the power that ritual has when rightly
held is similar to Jennifer's (of Wapato Island Farm), in that both
believe ceremony and ritual have value only insofar as they connect us
to the sacred in everyday life and help us live accordingly. In the modern
world, we are cut off from the moon to which the finger points, from the
mystery to which we all belong. Community ritual helps us reconnect
and live in harmony with the natural world and each other.

* * *

While rituals point to something that is larger than ourselves,
meaning-making practices are still nuanced and culturally specific.

They contain wisdom specific to a community that cannot simply be translated to a different context. Because of this, other people's rituals are not meant to be a smorgasbord for general consumption. There is a difference between drawing from the wisdom of other traditions and appropriating their rituals (though that line is not always clear).

In the United States, the most sacred Indigenous ceremonies were banned until the late 1970s. Prohibiting a people from participating in their own rituals was part of an attempted cultural genocide. This violence contributed to centuries of trauma and profound suffering that continues to this day. Reclamation of ceremony is important to the identity and collective healing of Indigenous peoples. Within this context, casually adopting Indigenous rituals is another version of the colonizer's mindset, taking what isn't ours.

Even if adopted with respectful intent, taking rituals outside of their original context reveals the borrower's misunderstanding of their unique potential and power. It places the importance of the ritual in the action itself rather than its ability to signal what lies beyond it. Hunger for the rituals of others suggests a lack of faith in our own ability to generate meaningful symbols or to live in a way that meets our heartfelt longings. If we don't align our perceptions and lifestyles to participate in rituals, they won't serve to get us there.

Rituals from other communities and cultures can and do get transmitted as shared traditions rather than appropriations. It is fortunate that we can meaningfully draw on symbols and practices that come from wisdom traditions other than those of our direct ancestors. Some of these traditions have a long and rich history of translation to other cultures. As a hybrid descendant of Western European cultures, I practice meditation in ways that are an amalgamation of more than one Eastern tradition, and not from my own ancestral traditions. My teachers, mostly Western themselves, studied for years with respected Eastern Buddhist teachers who conferred on them the status of teacher. The transmission of the dharma through training new generations of teachers continues in major spiritual centers in the United States, and includes a rigorous multiple-year curriculum, mentoring, and long periods of retreat.

● ● ●

Where do we live symbolically? Nowhere except
where we participate in the ritual of life.

—C. G. JUNG

It's an honor to be invited to witness other peoples' rituals and celebrations. I accept every invitation I can, watching as a guest and participating when invited. Learning about these traditions, the wisdom and beliefs behind them, enriches me, and I feel connected to those whose rituals I witness. The honor of the invitation can be returned by being respectfully and gratefully present. Respect and gratitude are shown in different ways within different cultures, so sometimes we need guidance.

Perhaps the symbols used in our rituals come from a shared collective unconscious, as Carl Jung believed. Or maybe, instead, they tap into the neural wiring that we all share that creates the experience of belonging and reverence. However rituals operate and whatever their origins, they work on our psyches in ways not often accessed in daily life (unless they are part of our everyday experience). Ritual and their symbols, rightly held, break down the too-often rigid boundary between our conscious and unconscious minds, between our intellect and embodied, intuited knowledge. And they hold the promise of breaking down the walls between us.

chapter 7

this being human is a guest house[1]

*After a pause she said, "I see your magic is not good
only for large things."*
*"Hospitality," he said, "kindness to a stranger, that's
a very large thing."*

—URSULA K. LE GUIN, *THE TOMBS OF ATUAN*

A Tradition of Welcoming Guests

In the modern world, the practice of hospitality—making room for the
guest—is not the elevated virtue it once was. Though now most often
associated with the service industry, hospitality is a meritorious practice with ancient roots in many cultures and faith traditions, and was
once viewed as a necessary pillar of civilization.

In true hospitality it doesn't matter who the guest is; the stranger
is treated in the same way as friends and family. The hosts provide for
physical needs as well as emotional ones, including food, shelter, and
companionship, expecting nothing in exchange. In hospitable cultures,
there is the understanding that everyone, at different times, will be both
host and stranger. The communities in this book offer inspiring models
of the art of making others feel welcome, intentionally making time to
meaningfully share their lives with guests.

When I think back on experiences that have stayed with me, what
stand out are times when I was welcomed as the stranger. Here is one
such memory that is more than two decades old: a friend and I were staying in a beautiful stone home in Papingo, Greece, nestled in the densely
forested Pindus mountain range in the region of Zagoria. The village's
unique, well-preserved architecture seemed like it belonged in a fairy tale.
In this place of a few hundred permanent residents, you were as likely to
see a cow walking down the stone paths as a human.

From Papingo we took a day trip to explore a few of the other
forty-five secluded villages and hamlets in this mountainous region.
Despite the region's stunning natural beauty, it receives few tourists.
We stopped at a tiny hamlet that appeared abandoned yet still cared
for, giving the experience a surreal feeling. Walking the cobblestone

streets without encountering a soul, we were about to leave when we saw a woman working a very small plot of land with her donkey.

She looked surprised to see us and exchanged a few words with my friend Lia, who spoke Greek (I do not). Her name was Ana, and she asked us to wait a few minutes while she put her donkey back in his shelter before taking us to her home. Lia protested, not wanting to disturb her at work, but she insisted. The homes were built close together and Ana led us down a few houses to her home, where she had us sit with her husband as she washed up from the fields. The inside of their home was simple and tidy. Her husband was shy, and we sat in polite silence waiting for Ana's return.

When Ana reappeared, not only had she washed up; she now had on a different, brightly colored head scarf and decorative apron over her clothes. And she had even put on lipstick. We were surprised by the lengths to which she had gone and expressed our delight, which she acknowledged with a modest smile. Ana set out a cheese pie she had made along with a few things preserved in jars. She told us that, aside from the two of them, there were only three other people living in this tiny hamlet—a widow and another elderly couple. Their children occasionally came, but there were few other visitors.

We visited for only a short time, maybe thirty minutes. She invited us to stay longer, but the conversation, mostly between Ana and Lia, had wound down. Ana's husband and I watched them speak with polite smiles fixed on our faces. Though Lia and I were ready to leave, we felt the time spent with this couple had been a small treasure. I wonder if it was the lovely hospitality that keeps Ana's face, headscarf, and bright lipstick vivid in my memory today.

The warmth of the experience of being unexpected guests who were received with such hospitality was a highlight of a trip that included many special moments. Lia later told me about the history of travelers passing through these villages, some providing services to these geographically isolated places. When the villages were livelier, they usually had community guesthouses or rooms set off from the church. Those staying overnight in the village would be invited into homes for meals and conversation. Although this isolated region has a long history of welcoming the stranger, hospitality has deep roots in Greek culture in general. *Xenia* is an ancient Greek concept of hospitality that is translated as *guest-friendship* or *ritualized friendship*.

Inviting the Stranger into Our World

When most people hear the word *hospitality* they think of the industry that provides paying guests with lodging, food and beverages, entertainment, or travel services. Because it is an industry, even a personal connection between host and guest is a transaction with an underlying profit motive. That's not to say that people within the hospitality industry are not genuinely hospitable; they are. Indeed, during the pandemic we saw generous displays of hospitality where these workers served communities in need. For example, when restaurants were shut down during the pandemic, many across the country teamed up with nonprofits in order to feed hospital employees and other frontline workers.

The genuine hospitality that is most needed, from all of us, is one that welcomes others into our personal lives and communities for nothing in return. This more radical welcome includes, even prioritizes, the stranger and those who are different from us.

Hospitality can take any form: a ride, a handwritten note, an attentive ear, rest or shelter. It manifests when we make something extra special with a guest in mind, such as a meal or a pretty setting at the table. Hospitality requires our presence and attention. In fact, in today's world, listening is often the most hospitable thing we can offer. Yet more than any particular action, hospitality is an internal state of openness toward those outside our everyday circles of care.

It is human nature to want to affiliate with people who are like us, yet hospitality requires that we include, and even prioritize, those whom we have never met before. True hospitality becomes possible when we examine our deep-seated preferences and understand which groups of people are outside our immediate circle of regard. The next step is to stretch our comfort levels and find a path to inviting in those on our personal margins.

The kind of welcome that is so needed today is one characterized by mutuality, where we are open to the possibility that those we invite in will change us. This is different from dependency or a handout, or charity where there is a hierarchy between the giver and receiver. And it is different from hospitality as a form of entertainment. In its highest form, hospitality breaks down the walls that separate us, nurturing the spirit of community and a sense of belonging in both host and guest.

Who are the people on our personal margins toward whom we could extend an invitation? They are those whose preferences and lifestyles make us uncomfortable—they love differently, think differently, look and sound different from us. They are our neighbors whom we recognize or greet on the street but have yet to sit down with and share personal stories. They include the homeless men and women in the parks and hidden places near where we live. They are in our workplaces, behind the counter serving us coffee, and even within our existing personal communities.

I first heard the phrase "people on our margins" from Stephanie Spellers,[2] an Episcopalian priest, in her book on radical welcome, where her focus is on small, personal gatherings. She intentionally moves her language away from the commonly used phrase "marginalized people" to "people on our margins," and this shift in emphasis is significant. It locates the margins as a place in our minds rather than within the person whom society, or individuals, puts there. This important shift places the responsibility on all of us to change the conditions that disenfranchise individuals and groups. The shift also gives us insight to help transform our habit of mind that categorizes things in ways that perpetuate the personal experience of separateness.

What would it look like if we committed to a lifestyle of hospitality? In order to find out, we must first create space in our schedules and lives for spontaneous invitations and lingering conversations. With time and a shift in priorities, we are freer to make choices that make us more hospitable, feeling more connected to each other in the process.

• • •

Hospitality is an orientation toward others where we extend invitations in a way that becomes habitual only when practiced. Kortney

Lawlor, a friend who worked for years in the hospitality business, has a real talent for paying attention to those around her and finding beautiful, considerate touches that make them feel welcome and special. "Hospitality has always been about creating community and a fast track to friendship," said Kortney. For her, a particularly painful part of the isolation caused by COVID-19 was the loss of spontaneity, such as not being able to invite friends over to share an unplanned meal.

She believes hospitality, like most things we value and aspire to, is a set of skills we learn. "We aren't taught that here," Kortney observed, meaning the United States. We spoke of countries we had visited, for example Mexico and Turkey, where hospitality is highly valued, part of everyday life, and so modeled for children.

Hospitality is a mindset, an attitude where what we have to offer right now is enough. We don't have to wait until we have a great idea, a gift for entertaining, or for the conditions to be just right. It helps to remember that it is our thoughtfulness and desire to connect, and not the end result, that are most important. And, not surprisingly, it is those who treat their guests well, like Kortney, who are often gracious guests, the qualities of which we'll discuss later on.

● ● ●

In a conversation I had with Ross Gay, an award-winning poet and author, he shared a story of the Bloomington Community Orchard, a nonprofit free-fruit-for-all justice project, that to him personifies hospitality:

> We had to tussle a little bit about whether or not to put a lock on the gate to the orchard. But people are nervous, you know? We've put in a million hours on this thing; we don't want it to get messed up. So there was this argument effectively about property and sharing and hospitality. And, as I see it, the orchard won. Because after much conversation it was decided that, no, there cannot be a lock on the gate to the community orchard. It is antithetical to the practice of hospitality in a way. It's not like we knew how [to be hospitable], but we were getting together to figure it out, and the last thing you do is put a lock on the gate.

*This story still moves me and strikes me as the most import-
ant thing about the orchard project, because it's about everyday
community. Tussling a little bit and asking ourselves, "How do
we want to do it?" And in the end people are adamant that the
gate has to be open.*

Creatively Sharing Community

All the communities in this book value genuine hospitality, wanting
others to share in the experience and the gifts that they offer to each
other. This doesn't mean that an invitation to membership is extended
to everyone, but they do find creative ways to share the gifts of their
communities.

COVID-19 of course wreaked havoc on our ability to welcome people
into our homes and community spaces. Not only were we unable to
extend invitations to others; we also experienced the loss of gathering among ourselves. Some communities found ways to modify their
welcome, meeting online or safely outdoors, whereas others hunkered
down until they could congregate as they had before the pandemic.

Volunteering within other communities is a great way to meaningfully participate in them, experiencing a sense of belonging while also
giving back. Too often, when people volunteer, they feel underused and
disconnected, experiencing their efforts as peripheral to the organization
or community. In contrast, vibrant communities believe relationships are
built while serving together, so they invest time and energy in creating
volunteer opportunities that provide such an experience.

From the very beginning, Community First! Village viewed volunteers as essential to its mission. It is easy to plug into their community
by going to its website and signing up for one of the variety of service
opportunities available: work side by side with neighbors at the on-site
farm tending gardens or caring for goats and chickens. Be part of the
community by taking a shift at the market that sells provisions as well
as artwork made by residents. Join one of the nineteen thousand volunteers with Mobile Loaves and Fishes on a monthly team that delivers
food and other items to people living on the streets.

Visitors are part of the energy in the village, and guests are welcome to enjoy the public spaces without committing as a volunteer. Austinites enjoy gathering for the popular Friday movie night, a free community event where visitors can support neighbors by purchasing food at the concessions. At the community market visitors can get provisions as well as art and crafts created by village artisans. While visiting, guests can drop off their vehicles at the Car Care for an oil change, wash, detailing, or state inspection. All proceeds for goods and services provided by people in the village who had once been homeless go directly to them. Those who want to have a more immersive experience can rent an Airstream or a tiny home at the Community Inn.

The spirit of the L'Arche community is experienced by the way it extends hospitality to guests at its 140 homes situated around the globe. Whether someone lives in the homes, is administrative staff, or is a friend of L'Arche, everyone is welcomed and can build relationships. Each L'Arche home creates its own unique ways to welcome people who want to participate in the community.

At the three L'Arche homes in Portland, Oregon, for example, opportunities include joining in a weekend yardwork party and helping prepare meals. For a more personal experience, volunteers can spend weekly one-on-one time with a house member, talking, listening to music, reading books aloud, or playing games.

COVID-19 made in-person gatherings with guests impossible, and community members struggled emotionally from being cut off from the outside world. But at the onset of the pandemic, L'Arche searched for resourceful, alternative ways to stay connected online. In Zoom gatherings, friends of L'Arche joined people in the homes to share music, games, and personal stories. The larger online group gatherings are interspersed with smaller breakout room activities that allow for more personal connection.

The Harmony Project in Columbus, Ohio, has a long waiting list to become part of the choir. Yet in the spirit of community, they post available opportunities on their social media, making it possible for anyone interested to connect via volunteering. For example, they reached out for volunteers to work virtually with high school seniors on their college admissions essays. Of course, everyone is invited to come to Harmony's biannual concerts and share the magic of community with friends and family. And Harmony posts YouTube video content, offering inspiring and concrete ideas for building stronger, more inclusive communities.

Farmers at Wapato Island Farm know that hard work, celebration, and building relationships go hand in hand. They have carved out space on Tuesday afternoons for anyone in the Portland area who wants to get their hands dirty and learn about plants. During that window of time, guests are also welcome to simply come sit on the land to be close to nature. If that time slot doesn't work, they can attend one of the farm's workshops offered throughout the year to learn about plants, mushrooms, and regenerative farming. People can also meet the farmers at one of several markets in Portland and buy the different herbal medicines cultivated and produced on the farm while learning about the medicinal uses of plants and fungi.

Radical Hospitality Respects Limits

Many people are so busy that they can't make enough time for family and friends, let alone people they have yet to meet. To be open to the stranger is a lot to ask of ourselves, but extending invitations need not leave us feeling depleted. It is important to discern the difference between stretching our limits and overextending them. That line is not always clear, and it shifts depending on what is happening within and around us and how our guests interact with us.

Just as in our personal worlds, extending hospitality is not always convenient for communities. Some visitors take more energy, especially those who are unfamiliar with the community's culture or unintentionally insensitive to its boundaries. Yet some of the most challenging guests are the ones most in need of an invitation to belong. Still, being hospitable to even the most skillful guests can be taxing if it's a bad time for us, one where we find it difficult to be open. It helps to be aware of our limits before extending an invitation. At the same time, the practice of hospitality requires that we create a lifestyle that is not chronically overly busy.

• • •

Jennifer Rose Marie Serna, the owner of Wapato Island Farm, had in the past extended an invitation to anyone interested to participate in rituals for the plants, for example one that coincided with the full moon. But she found that the experience left her feeling depleted. Participants sometimes took offerings made during the ritual, which were meant for the plants, back to their own homes as a way to remember the ritual. There was no selfish intent; they weren't aware of Indigenous gratitude practices. Jennifer concluded that offering this kind of ritual participation wasn't a good way for her to establish healthy boundaries.

She still offers access to the land and her teachings, and she tries to provide a container around these experiences by communicating about the notion of reciprocity. "Receiving is beautiful, sharing is beautiful. There needs to be both. . . . There needs to be an idea of an exchange," she explained.

The word *exchange* as Jennifer uses it reminds me of the concept of *dana* in Buddhism, which is the practice of cultivating generosity. In Buddhist tradition, the teachings—which are regarded as priceless—are offered freely. *Dana* is not payment for teaching services rendered; it is instead a gift from the heart. When we make a contribution to the teacher, we are supporting not just them but the entire community, including our own spiritual practice. Practicing *dana,* giving in gratitude for the teachings without expecting anything in return, is an important spiritual training that seeds the ground for other meritorious action.

Jennifer now provides more specific guidance for how to participate in gratitude practices. For example, the farm hosts a milky oats U-pick harvest in June. Milky oats are important in plant medicine; they can be used in tinctures or vinegar to support the nervous system. Anyone who wants to come pick the oats for their personal use can do so for free. Jennifer sends out the invitation on Instagram and the farm's website, along with a request: "We ask you to make an offering to the land. Examples are tobacco, a song, a stone, something special."

• • •

When communities welcome others to participate in some way, they should be sensitive to the needs of their membership. For example,

L'Arche homes around the world have a long tradition of welcoming visitors for meals and other activities. Some homes can accommodate overnight guests. House members, like everyone else, are tired at the end of their day and need to have say over who is in their personal space.

For example, before I visited a L'Arche home in Washington, DC, I reached out to Luke Smith, the executive director and community leader there, who then met with core members in one of the homes to see if they were interested in hosting an overnight guest and speaking with her about community. When they expressed interest and a date was set, Luke and I spoke again so he could familiarize me with daily life there and a little about the interests of each core member. I imagine he did this to create a framework so I could get the most out of my stay and, as importantly, to help me be an engaged, respectful guest of their hospitality.

The Skills of a Gracious Guest

For hospitality to serve as a bridge to authentic connection and a source of belonging, we need experiences as both the welcomer and the welcomed, host and guest. Just as the art of being a hospitable host requires a set of skills that are learned and practiced, so does being a gracious guest.

Those who welcome us by offering what they have—their time, effort, possessions, attention—are extending themselves and showing us that we matter. The invitation is a gift, and it is important to convey back to them that their interest in us is appreciated and that they, too, matter. In cultures where hospitality is highly valued, everyone is encouraged to develop the qualities of a good host: warmth, generosity, attentiveness. These customs can flourish because there is also an obligation for guests to be grateful and to value being hospitable themselves.

There are different ways to be a gracious guest, depending on the culture of the person extending the invitation. We might not always know how to show appreciation and respect in different contexts, and we will make mistakes along the way. We will be fine if we stay curious and humble, and we can always ask questions and take the lead from our hosts. If the host's culture is different from our own, doing some research beforehand is a good way to learn how appreciation is shown.

Some hallmarks of a good guest are to respond definitively to the invitation (so the host knows who will be there), show up on time, and receive what is offered with gratitude. It is not gracious to equivocate, sending the host the message that we are hedging so we can see what else might be happening. (Unfortunately, this kind of behavior is too common in cultures that are both overly committed and commitment averse.) Ways to show appreciation include bringing a thoughtful gift for the host, perhaps something they can enjoy later.

As a gracious guest, appreciation for hospitality gets tricky when, for example, the offering is a meal and we have dietary restrictions. While working in Africa years ago, my colleague and I were invited to dinner by generous hosts who served chicken, which they themselves could afford maybe twice a year. My colleague was vegetarian but did not tell our hosts beforehand. Once we arrived, she chose not to say that she did not eat meat, because the meal was a real sacrifice for our friends, and she wanted to honor their generosity. She ate a couple bites of chicken but could not continue. After a few minutes she told them that her stomach was off, which was the truth after eating meat for the first time in a long while, and she asked if she could take the rest home.

Today, as we have greater awareness of how food is sourced and its impact on health and the environment, more people are making changes to their diet. Many know someone who is vegetarian or vegan, or who is sensitive to gluten or has food allergies. As a result, more hosts are making at least one dish that is meat and dairy free, but they cannot keep track of everyone's dietary preferences. As a gracious guest, let the host know beforehand about any food restrictions, while at the same time offering to bring a dish to share. If the host is not told about food restrictions beforehand, don't bring it up during the meal, and eat the sides. If it is too late for the host to be able to accommodate, there is no need to shine the light on not being able to enjoy their efforts. We can take care of ourselves while honoring our hosts' hospitality by focusing on their generosity in bringing us together to connect around the table.

Many of us can probably think of times we've committed a faux pas in response to someone's hospitable gesture. Looking back, I remember times while traveling where I so enjoyed the hospitality offered that I probably overstayed my welcome. For example, while visiting a community in Columbus, Ohio, I discovered a shop of Turkish imports. The owner, who is from Istanbul, brought out wine, cheese, and dried fruit and shared stories about his country. I had time on my hands, so I lingered to enjoy the food and conversation for well over an hour. Although I bought beautiful things from his shop, the length of my stay didn't reflect an appreciation that he was working as other customers came through the store. I continued to encourage him to share more stories of Istanbul, and he obliged. In hindsight, and reflecting on other hospitable experiences I have had while in Turkey, I recognized that he may have been too polite not to oblige me. If I found myself in a similar situation again, I would offer to leave when the shop became busy.

Being a gracious guest mirrors the qualities of a hospitable host, receptivity and generosity, foundations for building lasting relationships.

"From Her Beacon-Hand Glows World-Wide Welcome"

When I was writing about the practice of hospitality, my thoughts kept returning to the national conversation around refugees and other people seeking to work and live in this country. The United States's disastrous immigration policy and our lack of ability or will to reform it reflect a fearful and inhospitable stance toward those who are seeking help and want to belong here. The words of poet Emma Lazarus, enshrined in an inscription on the pedestal of the Statue of Liberty, are a call to welcome those who seek refuge on our shores, an important part of our history that rejects a nationalist identity. Reflecting upon traditions of hospitality can help us create more inclusive, welcoming, and mutually beneficial immigration policies.

According to UN data, the United States hosts roughly one-fifth of migrants worldwide, and refugees account for a small but growing percentage of that group.[3] This is a fact and is not going to change regardless of our feelings about it. The openness or restrictiveness of policy is more shaped by immediate economic circumstances and political ideology than by a deeper understanding of the forces underlying migration. What guides US policy often thwarts our own economic interests, and channels to coming here legally remain long, convoluted, and expensive.[4]

What prevents us from having more permeable boundaries that enable easier access for people to legally enter, while having open and intelligent conversations around the limits of hospitality? The primary impediment is our inability to hold tension and have dialogue that makes room for differences. All we hear coming at us is *yes* or *no* to immigration. The conversations that lead to real solutions remain uninitiated, so the positions getting public airtime are extreme or unhelpful: ugly, xenophobic views on the one hand, a call for borders as boundaries to be entirely abolished on the other, and nonspecific calls for reform in the middle.

As the world faces historically high levels of displacement, we must better prepare our borders to accommodate unexpected guests. People who have lost everything from violence and other catastrophes need safety and help regaining the capacity to direct their own lives. In addition, the United States has always relied upon guest workers from different countries. Because we cannot hash out a coherent process to allow them to enter legally, at least on a temporary basis, they come in ways that place them at high risk for abuse. We see this in images of children and their parents being detained in cages and other inhumane conditions. Hidden from view is how employers frequently exploit their workers, people with no redress because of their undocumented status.

● ● ●

Sonia Shah's book *The Next Migration: The Beauty and Terror of Life on the Move* explores how migration has always been the norm and is encoded in our bodies. The book disputes inaccurate yet persistently held biases about people who migrate. She writes, "For centuries, we've suppressed the fact of the migration instinct, demonizing it as a harbinger of terror. We've constructed a story about our past, our bodies, and the natural world in which migration is the anomaly. It's an illusion. And once it falls, the entire world shifts."[5]

The view that people belong in a fixed place persists because of an erroneous belief that people are biologically distinct and should not mix. Shah's research presents clear evidence that human mobility has always been the norm; for example, people crossed oceans by canoe long before Western civilization. The idea that long-distance migration requires modern technology is inaccurate. Shah describes the long history of the Western "natural order" bias, which is the notion that historically, humans lived separately in isolation—a view even advocated by scientists for nearly two centuries until they looked more closely and saw that they were wrong.

People who continue to peddle xenophobic views are now packaging them as warnings about "caravans" of intruders at our border, urging the loss of civil liberties under the guise of protecting civilians from this threat. This lie persists despite evidence to the contrary. In the United States, crime rates are actually lower among undocumented immigrants than among US citizens,[6] and in nine of the ten cities that received the most refugees relative to their size, their safety improved.[7]

The fearmongers also seek to perpetuate the myth that those seeking refuge are "illegal aliens" who are takers rather than contributors. On the contrary, history has repeatedly shown that new immigrants, who often do require help upon arrival, replenish our communities within a half generation with vitality, skills, and resources. As an example, Shah cites a National Academy of Sciences report showing that immigrants cost the US economy $57.4 billion between 2011 and 2013, their children added a $30.5 billion net benefit, and their grandchildren contributed $223.8 billion![8]

Shah's central message is that we can reclaim the truth of our collective history of welcoming migration and shift the current crisis into creative solutions. But she warns that if the inevitable migration due to climate change continues to be cast as a catastrophic disaster, we will be ill-prepared and miss an opportunity to meet the future from a position of compassionate strength.

Hospitable immigration policies for workers and refugees are smart and advantageous for everyone already living in the United States. A smooth transition of immigrant workers in areas where there is a short-age of labor will economically benefit the entire country. And we have the capacity to welcome more refugees, a number that has been reduced to unprecedented lows, even as communities across the country stand ready to welcome them.

Whatever our differences on how permeable the borders should be and how to direct policy on immigration, nothing must prevent us from adopting a more hospitable stance toward everyone who seeks refuge, work, or a new life here.

◦ ◦ ◦

How do we begin to talk about something as complex as immigration in our personal communities when we are lacking healthy models for it in the national conversation? We don't have to be experts on the topic in order to have meaningful conversations about it, and we can learn more together. Not only is it possible to have open dialogues around potentially charged topics; it is healthy. But it is near impossible to navigate these conversations when the focus is exclusively on our differences or, conversely, when we avoid our differences in order to keep the peace.

It is in our communities where we can make room for expressing our differences without falling into a false equivalency trap, the place where the national dialogue is stuck. For example, the false equivalency trap for those who want unlimited asylum (or closed borders) might be expressed as something like, "If you are hospitable [or want a safe country], then you will think about immigration exactly as I do."

Conversations within our communities start where there is an agreed-upon value—here, hospitality—with an understanding that issues are complex and that we will have differences about what that looks like. Focus on what community members have in common, because that is the basis on which to build. The first step to navigating a potentially charged topic is to agree to listen carefully to what each person holds dear, or the values underlying their positions. Recognize that when it comes to listening, everyone in the group has room for improvement. Witness and appreciate everyone's efforts to open themselves up beyond their current comfort level, no matter where they are starting from.

A helpful question to ask is, "What are your hopes and concerns for your community or your country?" This kind of question helps us understand the underlying values someone holds. If someone wants more restricted borders than we do, maybe it is because of a concern for safety and security. If so, we can validate the desire for safety and maybe draw comparisons to others with similar concerns—people who may have even more skin in the game. For example, migrants coming from Latin America are also motivated by safety concerns, wanting an opportunity to leave behind dangerous cartels or economic devastation.

When there is common ground, identify it and pause, rather than jumping to a "yes but" response. Only when we know we are understood and can recognize common ground can we then move to a deeper conversation about our differences. A lesson from the circles of dialogue on racism in chapter 5 is that trust building takes time, and we need to be willing to sit down more than once. If we find ourselves going down a rabbit hole of polarized views, it's time to take another pause and try to return to a place where we can relate to each other. A pause is not avoidance but a recognition that we can only move forward at the speed where we can still maintain some level of trust.

● ● ●

In our personal communities, in addition to sharing the stories of our own migrant backgrounds, we can become curious about the experiences of those living near us who have their own valuable stories to share. Bridging the refugee experience to a shared, personal story helps us relate to an actual person, which can ignite our compassion. Within our personal communities we might research the cultures of different immigrant communities living near us. Activity might be structured around a shared experience, like planning a collective meal featuring recipes from the countries of more recent immigrant neighbors. As a group, our communities might find activities that introduce us to our neighbors and their cultures.

Within our communities, let's share positive stories of the contributions of the immigrants and refugees living near us. Many of us have our own similar immigrant origin stories, ones where our ancestors worked hard and did without in order to give their children and future generations opportunity. People who come to this country are often leaving behind difficult circumstances, but they bring with them cultures and traditions that enhance our own. When we practice hospitality by welcoming as guests those in need of hospitality, we make friends and strengthen the fabric of our own communities.

vibrant community is ever evolving

Maybe making those to whom we are kind our kin. To whom, even, those we might be. And that circle is big.

—ROSS GAY, from "Pulling Carrots," in *The Book of Delights: Essays*[1]

Placing Our Gaze and Caring Each Other Through

Poet Ross Gay shared with me how, for him, the word *joy* is evolving to mean something like "the feeling that emerges in the midst of our caring each other through our sorrows." As we spoke together, we found ourselves coming back multiple times to the notion of care as a practice. These expressions of nontransactional relationship, which are the very heart of vibrant community, are all around us and always in play.

"The idea of care wasn't my idea," said Ross. "It flew into my head along with the instruction to write every day about something that delights me." He would take note and pay attention to the little things, and then pay attention to the accrual of these little things, "which is in fact your life," he said. For him the *practice* element of care is essential, and although he balks at giving advice, he will say this much: "Start with what you love. Study what you love." Tending to what we love by paying close attention to it is, for him, the practice of delight and joy, and community.

Ross shared a personal story of community to illustrate how his understanding of caring for each other has evolved over time. The community he's speaking of began with the orchard project initiated in 2010 in Bloomington, Indiana, a small university city where Ross lives and teaches.

Amy Countryman, who is now his neighbor and dear friend, placed an ad in the local newspaper announcing a meeting for anyone interested in creating a community orchard. She did this as part of her undergraduate thesis on food insecurity, after her thesis director suggested that she talk to Lee Huss, Bloomington's urban forester at the time. Lee agreed to set aside an acre of land and $2,000 in seed money for the project if Amy could show community interest and support. Ross, who heard about the meeting through a friend, went to the first gathering of about a hundred people, none of whom he knew at the time.

A spirit of collaboration was present in that very first meeting, where people spontaneously broke into teams to generate ideas on how to create the community orchard, a new experience for them all. Ross recalled that there were multiple generations in attendance, including elders who knew more about gardening, people "deep in the woods of the biology of plants," and those who knew how to dig a hole.

For Ross, this was a wonderful project because a bunch of people joined together with the common goals of learning and sharing. They worked hard to make a physical space where they could practice this thing called community. Strangers to him when the project began, in the process of laboring toward a dream together they became "like deep beloveds." By this he means, "if something happened to any of them and they needed to have a place for their kids to land, the answer would be 'of course!'"

This is vibrant community: it starts with an invitation, an idea, or a project, and organically unfolds as people say *yes* and show up to make it happen, caring about each other in the process.

● ● ●

It pays to be intentional about where we place our gaze, as that then is our guide, steering us in the direction we want to go. When we cultivate the spirit of vibrant community by developing practices such as those offered up in this book, we participate in a new paradigm of belonging. It is a deeply meaningful path where we as authentic individuals choose to prioritize the good of the whole.

● ● ●

Whether we experience it to be true or not, we do belong right now, just as we are. Yet we also exist in a world where narratives of separateness dominate, and we often experience our belonging as conditional. The world of rigid categories casts a powerful spell, and we can stand in the doorway of unconditional belonging, afraid to step across the threshold because of our uncertainty about what lies on the other side. By cultivating the qualities of vibrant community in our lives, we better understand the pain of our separateness, and we find courage to commit to an interconnected way of living.

Belonging is not static; it is an internal state we can tap into, a sense of home not tied to physical place, though we experience it by showing up in real time and space. In vibrant communities we linger, labor, and listen; we grieve, heal, and find joy; and we practice connection in ways that radiate out beyond our personal boundaries. We build these places over time, and as we do, we get a taste of an emerging collective mindset that fundamentally challenges a version of social reality that is painfully limited in its notions of relationship and worth.

Protecting the Deep Longing to Belong

The need to belong—experienced as feeling understood, appreciated, and supported within close relationships—is a powerful motivator for our life choices. Our collective longing to belong is neither healthy nor unhealthy, though the ways in which we fulfill it have significant consequences for both our personal and our collective well-being.

Throughout this book, the word *vibrant* is used to characterize communities that generate the experience of healthy belonging, encouraging individuality and authenticity while sharing and working toward the common good.

Vibrant communities are healthy ones, though the embodiment of health exists on a continuum and is ever evolving. Healthy communities are self-reflective; they examine their assumptions and beliefs that both promote and inhibit living out their core values. They acknowledge mistakes in order to move beyond them, as they write the script for a new paradigm for how we relate to each other.

The qualities laid out in this book, when practiced, protect against harmful group dynamics, such as unhealthy conformity, where expressions of difference are discouraged, and the creation of an us vs. them dynamic that treats those outside the group as inferior or threats. When communities are built on trusting relationships, and the differences between people are welcome, divergent points of view are perceived not as a threat but as necessary. This is why it is so important for communities to adopt the skills to hold tension and handle conflict as it arises.

Solidarity comes out of our recognition of interdependence. A belief in the ties that bind us together strengthens our sense of belonging more than aligning against others ever has. The practice of hospitality expands our experience of solidarity and extends the circle of care outward beyond a community's boundaries.

There are paradoxes and tensions in living an authentic life. A tension we navigate within community is how to fulfill our personal needs and desires while maintaining a strong sense of responsibility to the whole. A paradox of community is that even though communities are generators of true belonging, we can access the same experience anytime, anywhere, because it is within us. When we really understand that our fundamental nature is one of connection, then a purposeful life is one where we promote connection in all our relationships, human and otherwise.

Vibrant communities practice a form of care that honors our differences while always recognizing our common humanity. The better we learn to care and to honor, the more we will feel a burning desire to live in ways that liberate not only all humans, but all living things. The practice of care must extend to the more-than-human world, to the earth that nurtures us all. Our communities are dependent on the health of the planet, and we can no longer continue to deplete the earth and its species and remain vibrant ourselves. When our communities treat each other as gifts and practice the kind of care where we are responsible for each other, extending that loving care to all beings, we will live in reciprocity and experience the abundance of belonging like never before.

● ● ●

Communities, like the individuals within them, must continuously evolve if they are to stay vibrant. Those you have met in this book are always in process, living the experience of connection and reflecting on ways to embody their values. The process is imperfect, at times uncomfortable and even conflictual, yet necessary for the health of the community.

A vibrant community twenty years ago looked different from how it looks today, and today it looks different from how it will look twenty years from now. We must focus on where we are heading, which requires reconciling with the past. In our communities, we are called to meet the challenges and opportunities of this moment in history. This begins by finding means to heal the rifts between us, cocreating language that builds connection, and joining each other across our differences.

Foundational change takes a long, long time and can only happen when we collectively take ongoing, meaningful action in the right direction. A fundamental shift in perceptions, in how we hold power, in what we see as most important, is inevitably gradual and at times disruptive. Sometimes we must call out stagnation and actions that take us backward. Still, what's most important for paradigmatic change is that we bear the disruption with solidarity, identifying and sharing stories of change in the direction of growth, and viewing ourselves as participants in the creation of powerful new stories.

Over five decades ago, when Martin Luther King Jr. gave a speech in acceptance of his Nobel Peace Prize, he spoke about a dynamic juncture that we still find ourselves in today. Now we are in a position to further the paradigmatic shift he foresaw, a freedom movement spreading toward wider liberation, nurtured by the spirit of vibrant community:

> In spite of the tensions and uncertainties of this period something meaningful is taking place. Old systems of exploitation and oppression are passing away, and out of the womb of a frail world new systems of justice and equality are being born. . . . Here and there an individual or group dares to love, and rises to the majestic heights of moral maturity. So in a sense this a great time to be alive.

The Invisible Web Connects Us All

After living in Brooklyn, New York, for most of my adult life, I now call the Pacific Northwest home. Part of my daily ritual is a walk among towering trees, occasionally including pockets of old-growth forest—Douglas fir, cedar, and hemlock—whose strength and stillness quiet the mind and invite reflection. However, it's the invisible web beneath my feet that now evokes the same awe I felt as a child while looking up at the night sky in a planetarium show. There I experienced an inkling of just how vast the universe is, feeling both connected to it all and infinitesimal, and uncomfortable with what felt like an irreconcilable contradiction.

We humans are often awed by the colossal trees that draw our eyes upward, with less appreciation for the majesty of the complex systems below us, working in ways our minds can touch but not fully fathom.

Subterranean mycelium networks, which we notice above ground as mushrooms, fungus, and white patches on the soil, have an intimate relationship with nearly all the earth's plant life. Within forests, these networks help distribute nutrients to the entire ecosystem of trees—the young, the scrappy ones, as well as those that tower above. Each tree's connection to the whole, and the whole forest's ability to nourish the more vulnerable among them, strengthens the entire ecosystem. This vast matrix also helps trees communicate among themselves and with different species of plants to enable the forest to adapt to changing conditions.

These extraordinarily complex networks of mutual collaboration exist not only in forests but everywhere there is life on land.[2] Although scientists have studied plant communication for nearly a century, the shift in focus to this contiguous life-giving network of mutuality is very recent by scientific standards. Until then, the favored view was that of competition between species instead of collaboration, the scientific gaze informed by a perceptual mindset of hierarchy and dominance.

When scientist Suzanne Simard set out as a young researcher to study collaboration and mutuality in old-growth forests, a framework influenced by the ways of Indigenous peoples, she received little support. Her findings, published in the prestigious journal *Nature* in the late 1990s, were received with some enthusiasm but also sharp criticism from the scientific establishment. The controversial focus on connection over competition, and her willingness to challenge the prevailing view, made it difficult for her to get funding for her research, and at one point she almost gave up.[3] Now her work is well respected within the scientific community, even as there are still different points of view. The findings of her body of work affirm what many of us intuit from our experience of deep connection when we spend time in nature: we are in this together.

● ● ●

A vast network of unseen life-sustaining connectivity is an apt metaphor for how vibrant communities are incubators for a healthy ecosystem of belonging among humans, and between humans and all other living things.

Imagine how our own perceptions would change, our imaginations would ignite, if we trained our gaze on models of relating where humans worked together, finding joy in sharing. We would restore the balance between the forces of collaboration and competition whose gross imbalance has led to toxic division, social inequality, and a depletion of natural resources. Healthy competition is possible only when collaboration is the most respected and valued norm, and when we have the eyes to recognize and lift up efforts that creatively use the gifts of all. When we study—and love—collaboration over competition, we can attain outcomes that far surpass accomplishments stemming from an individualistic mindset.

Transformation occurs when we commit our attention, time, and resources to the greatest force of change, which is unity through connection, cultivated through practices of healthy belonging within our communities. The practices of true belonging are those that nurture care, acceptance, diversity, an appreciation of different views, celebration and ritualization of daily life and our values, and hospitality toward people outside our communities.

Vibrant communities help us navigate the inevitable contradictions that sometimes arise in pursuing our personal interests while prioritizing the well-being of everyone. In vibrant communities we grapple with the challenge of how to honor our traditions while cocreating new ones with others who have their own treasured heritages, because respect for different paths toward shared goals is our best chance for success. Communities that practice the skills that make room for differences are the incubators in which we nurture our common humanity. They are where we learn and practice in-group cooperation as the necessary foundation for between-group collaboration. And they are places where we reflect upon this moment in history and are willing to take an honest inventory of our past, the light and the shadows, to create a healthier future.

As more people commit attention and resources to building vibrant communities, there will be more ways for everyone to join and experience the benefits. Through ongoing effort within our personal communities, a confluence of cultures of care will generate a collective energy that will tip the scales, allowing us to meet the enormous challenges we face with purpose and joy.

Right now, we can commit to a life where we relate to each other from an understanding that we belong, and we belong to each other. Making vibrant community central to our lives is no small undertaking, yet it is our greatest hope, revolutionary in that it will create an unstoppable force of care and ingenuity, birthed in human connection.

notes

introduction: a crisis in belonging

1 Holt-Lunstad, J., Smith, T. B., & Layton, J. B. (2010). Social relationships and mortality risk: A meta analytic review. *PLoS Medicine,* *7*(7), e1000316. https://doi.org/10.1371/journal.pmed.1000316

2 Eccles, J. S., & Roeser, R. W. (2011). Schools as developmental contexts during adolescence. *Journal of Research on Adolescence,* *21*(1), 225–241. https://doi.org/10.1111/j.532-7795.2010.00725.x

3 Lambert, N. M., Stillman, T. F., Hicks, J. A., Kamble, S., Baumeister, R. F., & Fincham, F. D. (2013). To belong is to matter: Sense of belonging enhances meaning in life. *Personality and Social Psychology Bulletin.* https://doi.org/10.1177/0146167213499186

4 Cigna U.S. Loneliness Index: Survey of 20,000 Americans examining behaviors driving loneliness in the United States (2018). https://www.cigna.com/static/www-cigna-com/docs/about-us/newsroom/studies-and-reports/combatting-loneliness/cigna-2020-loneliness-factsheet.pdf

5 Weinberger, A. H., Gbedemah, M., Martinez, A. M., Nash, D., Galea, S., & Goodwin, R. D. (2018). Trends in depression prevalence in the USA from 2005 to 2015: Widening disparities in vulnerable groups. *Psychological Medicine,* *48*(8). https://doi.org/10.1017/S0033291717002781

6 Hards, E., Loades, M., Higson-Sweeney, N., et al. (2021). Loneliness and mental health in children and adolescents with pre-existing mental health problems: A rapid systemic review. *British Journal of Clinical Psychology.* https://www.doi.org/10.1111/bjc.12331

7 National Academies of Sciences, Engineering, and Medicine. (2020). *Social isolation and loneliness in older adults: Opportunities for the health care system.* National Academies Press.

8 Putnam, R. D. (2000). *Bowling alone: The collapse and revival of American community.* Simon and Schuster.

9 Rubenstein, P. (2020, February 4). *How the wellness industry is taking over travel.* BBC Online. https://www.bbc.com/worklife/article/20200203-how-the-wellness-industry-is-taking-over-travel

10 Gerszberg, C. O. (2019, December 6). My week of 'noble silence.' *New York Times.* https://www.nytimes.com/2019/12/06/travel/silent-meditation-retreat.html

11 Cao, J. (2009). The analysis of tendency of transition from collectivism to individualism in China. *Cross-Cultural Communication, 5*(4), 42–52.

12 Westley, D. (1992). *Good things happen: Experiencing community in small groups.* Twenty-Third Publications.

chapter 1: a revolution of the heart

1 Lorde, A. (1984). The master's tools will never dismantle the master's house. In *Sister outsider: Essays and speeches.* Crossing Press, 112.

2 Roth, M. S. (2019, August 29). Don't dismiss 'safe spaces.' *New York Times.* https://www.nytimes.com/2019/08/29/opinion/safe-spaces-campus.html

3 Yang, L. (2015). Awakening together. *Inquiring Mind, 31*(2). https://www.inquiringmind.com/article/3102_12_yang_3-awakening-together/

4 HarmonyProjectOnline. (2013). South High Harmony [Video]. YouTube. www.youtube.com/watch?v=QLJgNwjmC2k

5 Ross, C. (2016). Exploring ways art and culture intersect with public safety: Identifying current practice and opportunities for further inquiry. Urban Institute/ArtPlace America.

6 HarmonyProjectOnline (2013). The Harmony Project: One week, one neighborhood, one Columbus [Video]. YouTube. www.youtube.com/watch?v=LZO-4Axv3xM

7 Ibid.

8 Ibid.

9 Moorman, T. (2019). Community project gives hope at Faith Mission. *Columbus Underground.* https://columbusunderground.com /community-project-gives-hope-at-faith-mission-tm1

10 Lieberman, A., & Schroeder, J. (2020). Two social lives: How differences between online and offline interaction influence social outcomes. *Current Opinion in Psychology, 31,* 16–21.

11 Hunt, M. G., Marx, R., Lipson, C., & Young, J. (2018). No more FOMO: Limiting social media decreases loneliness and depression. *Journal of Social and Clinical Psychology, 37*(10), 751–768.

12 Hiley, C. (2021). How much of your time is screen time? *Uswitch.* https://www.uswitch.com/mobiles/screentime-report/

13 Contreras, B. (2022, March 16). California bill would let parents sue social media companies for addicting kids. *Los Angeles Times.* https://www.latimes.com/business/technology/story/2022-03-16 /california-bill-would-let-parents-sue-social-media-companies -for-addicting-kids

chapter 2: a common commitment to care

1 Foster Wallace, D. (2009). *This is water: Some thoughts, delivered on a significant occasion, about living a compassionate life.* Little, Brown, and Company.

2 Bierman, K. L., Torres, M. M., Domitrovich, C. E., Welsh, J. A., & Gest, S. D. (2009) Behavioral and cognitive readiness for school: Cross-domain associations for children attending Head Start. *Social Development, 18*(2), 305–323.

3 Warneken, F., & Tomasello, M. (2006). Altruistic helping in human infants and young chimpanzees. *Science, 311*(5765), 1301–1303.

4 Stewart, M., Belle Brown, J., Donner, A., McWhinney, I. R., Oates, J., Weston, W., et al. (2000). The impact of patient-centered care on outcomes. *Journal of Family Practice, 49*(9), 796–804.

5 Amendolair, D. (2012). Caring behaviors and job satisfaction. *JONA: The Journal of Nursing Administration, 42*(1), 34–39.

6 Seppälä, E., & Cameron, K. (2015). Proof that positive work cultures are more productive. *Harvard Business Review*. https://hbr .org/2015/12/proof-that-positive-work-cultures-are-more -productive

7 Davis, C. (2021, May 21). *HMIS snapshot: Homelessness prevalence estimate* [Press release]. https://www.austinecho.org/blog /2021/05/21/11430/

8 Mobile Loaves and Fishes (2019). Richard's story: Connected to community [Video]. YouTube. https://www.youtube.com /watch?v=MohZyqYOZKQ

chapter 3: the vulnerable help us shed our masks

1 American Psychiatric Association. (2021). *What is intellectual disability?* https://www.psychiatry.org/patients-families/intellectual -disability/what-is-intellectual-disability

2 Centers for Disease Control and Prevention. (2018, August 16). *CDC: 1 in 4 US adults live with a disability* [Press release]. https:// www.cdc.gov/media/releases/2018/p0816-disability.html

3 Tippett, K. (Host). (2020, December 23). Gaelynn Lea's voice and violin [Audio podcast episode]. In *On being with Krista Tippett*. https://onbeing.org/programs/gaelynn-leas-voice-and-violin/

4 Ibid.

5 Ibid.

6 Ibid.

7 L'Arche USA. (2020, February 22). *Summary report from L'Arche International.* https://www.larcheusa.org/news_article /summary-report-from-larche-international/

8 L'Arche International. (2020). *Second stage charter process.* https://www.larche.org/documents/10181/2857344/CHA-Charter -process-guide_Stage2_200623_EN.pdf/f311497e-09ea-425f-a3ee -3a803e0c5563

9 L'Arche USA. (2020, February 22). *Summary report from L'Arche International.* https://www.larcheusa.org/the-way-forward/

chapter 4: inclusion is a spiritual practice

1 Lade, S. J., Walker, B. H., & Haider, L. J. (2020). Resilience as pathway diversity: Linking systems, individual, and temporal perspectives on resilience. *Ecology and Society, 25*(3). https://www.ecologyandsociety.org/vol25/iss3/art19/

2 Baggio, J. A., Freeman, J., Coyle, T. R., Nguyen, T. T., Hancock, D., Elpers, K. E., et al. (2019). The importance of cognitive diversity for sustaining the commons. *Nature Communications, 10*(875). https://doi.org/10.1038/s41467-019-08549-8

3 Yale University. (2018, May 24). What makes us well? Diversity, health care, and public transit matter. *ScienceDaily.* www.sciencedaily.com/releases/2018/05/180524174601.htm

4 Glieg, A. (2019). *American dharma: Buddhism beyond modernity.* Yale University Press.

5 Lorde, A. (2007). *Sister outsider: Essays and speeches.* Crossing Press.

6 Goldstein, J. (2014, December 9). Reflections on race and diversity (Recorded talk). Dharma Seed. https://www.dharmaseed.org/talks/25655/

7 Gleig, A. (2019). Undoing whiteness in American Buddhist modernism: Critical, collective, and contextual turns. In G. Yancy and E. McRae (Eds.), *Buddhism and whiteness: Critical reflections (Philosophy of race).* Lexington Books, 21–42.

8 Welwood, J. (2002). *Toward a psychology of awakening: Buddhism, psychotherapy, and the path of personal and spiritual transformation.* Shambhala.

9 Rubin Museum. (2019, March 22). Gina Sharpe + Roshi Pat Enkyo O'Hara + Dr. Pilar Jennings: Spiritual authority: Its abuses and uses [Video]. YouTube. https://www.youtube.com/watch?v=yR4W3niEleo

10 Nhat Hanh, T. (2014). *The art of communicating.* Harper One.

11 Zhang, H., Watson-Singleton, N. N., Pollard, S. E., Pittman, D. M., Lamis, D. A., Fischer, N. L., et al. (2019). Self-criticism and depressive symptoms: Mediating role of self-compassion. *OMEGA — Journal of Death and Dying, 80*(2), 202–223.

12 Chan, K. K. S., Yung, C. S. W., & Nie, G. M. (2020). Self-compassion buffers the negative psychological impact of stigma stress on sexual minorities. *Mindfulness, 11*. https://self-compassion.org/wp-content /uploads/2020/08/Chan2020.pdf

13 Lui, S., Li, C-I., Wang, C., Wei, M., & Ko, S. (2019). Self-compassion and social connectedness buffering racial discrimination on depression among Asian Americans. *Mindfulness, 11*(10), 672–682.

14 Neff, K., & Germer, C. (2018). *The mindful self-compassion workbook: A proven way to accept yourself, build inner strength, and thrive.* Guilford Press.

chapter 5: transforming tension into possibility

1 Zotigh, D. (2018). Native perspectives on the 40th anniversary of the American Indian Religious Freedom Act. *Smithsonian Magazine.* https://www.smithsonianmag.com/blogs/national-museum -american-indian/2018/11/30/native-perspectives-american -indian-religious-freedom-act/

2 *The Medicine Quilt* is available for purchase from Archway Publishing at   https://www.archwaypublishing.com/en/bookstore/bookdetails /768605-the-medicine-quilt.

chapter 6: ritual connects us to each other while pointing beyond

1 National Park Service. (n.d.). *Sauvie Island and the Hudson's Bay Company: Ft. Vancouver National Historic Site.* https://www .nps.gov/articles/sauvieisland.htm

chapter 7: this being human is a guest house

1 Rumi. (2004). *The guest house* (C. Barks, Trans.). Penguin Classics.

2 Spellers, S. (2021). *Radical welcome: Embracing God, the other, and the spirit of transformation.* Morehouse Publishing.

3 Coaston, J. (Host). (2021, October 13). America is "terrorizing" these workers: Migrant workers in America are in limbo. It's time to change things [Audio podcast episode]. In *The Argument*. https:// www.nytimes.com/2021/10/13/opinion/biden-immigration -migrant-workers.html

4 Ibid.

5 Shah, S. (2020). *The next great migration: The beauty and terror of life on the move*. Bloomsbury Publishing.

6 Light, M. T., He, J., & Robey, J. P. (2020). Comparing crime rates between undocumented immigrants, legal immigrants, and native-born U.S. citizens in Texas. *Proceedings of the National Academy of Sciences of the United States of America, 117*(51), 32340–32347.

7 New American Economy Research Fund. (2017). *Is there a link between refugees and U.S. crime rates? Examining crime data for the U.S. cities most impacted by resettlement from 2006– 2015*. https://research.newamericaneconomy.org/report/is-there -a-link-between-refugees-and-u-s-crime-rates/

8 National Academies of Sciences, Engineering, and Medicine. (2017). *The economic and fiscal consequences of immigration*. National Academies Press. https://doi.org/10.17226/23550

chapter 8: vibrant community is ever evolving

1 Gay, R. (2019). *The book of delights: Essays*. Algonquin Books.

2 Jabr, F. (2020, December 2). The social life of forests. *New York Times Magazine*. https://www.nytimes.com/interactive/2020 /12/02/magazine/tree-communication-mycorrhiza.html

3 Banks, K. (2021, March 24). Suzanne Simard overcame adversity to unlock the secret world of trees. *UA/AU: University Affairs/ Affaires universitaires*. https://www.universityaffairs.ca/features /feature-article/suzanne-simard-overcame-adversity-to-unlock -the-secret-world-of-trees/

further reading

Birdsong, M. (2020). *How we show up: Reclaiming family, friendship, and community.* Hachette Go.

Block, P. (2018). *Community: The structure of belonging.* Berrett-Koehler Publishers.

Gay, R. (2019). *The book of delights: Essays.* Algonquin Books.

Graham, A. (with L. Hall). (2017). *Welcome homeless: One man's journey of discovering the meaning of home.* W Publishing Group.

hooks, b. (2008). *Belonging: A culture of place.* Routledge.

Kimmerer, R. W. (2013). *Braiding sweetgrass: Indigenous wisdom, scientific knowledge, and the teaching of plants.* Milkweed Editions.

King Jr., M. L. (1968). *Where do we go from here: Chaos or community?* Beacon Press.

LaDuke, W. (2016). *Recovering the sacred: The power of naming and claiming.* Haymarket Books.

maree brown, a. (2017). *Emergent strategy: Shaping change, changing worlds.* AK Press.

Martin, C. E. (2016). *The new better off: Reinventing the American dream.* Seal Press.

Palmer, P. (2014). *Healing the heart of democracy: The courage to create a politics worthy of the human spirit.* Jossey-Bass.

Parker, P. (2020). *The art of gathering: How we meet and why it matters.* Riverhead Books.

Peck, M. S. (1987). *The different drum: Community making and peace.* Touchstone.

Prechtel, M. (2015). *The smell of rain on dust: Grief and praise.* North Atlantic Books.

Rani Jha, S. (2017). *Transforming communities: How people like you are healing their neighborhoods*. Chalice Press.

Shah, S. (2020). *The next great migration: The beauty and terror of life on the move*. Bloomsbury Publishing.

Talent, S., & Domela, P. (Eds.). (2012). *The unexpected guest: Art, writing, and thinking on hospitality*. Art Books Publishing.

Tsing, A. L. (2017). *The mushroom at the end of the world: On the possibility of life in capitalist ruins*. Princeton University Press.

Turner, T. (2017). *Belonging: Remembering ourselves home*. Her Own Room Press.

Vogl, C. (2016). *The art of community: Seven principles for belonging*. Berrett-Koehler Publishers.

Walker, A. (2006). *We are the ones we have been waiting for: Inner light in the time of darkness*. New Press.

Wheatley, M., & Frieze, D. (2011). *Walk out walk on: A learning journey into communities daring to live the future now*. Berrett-Koehler Publishers.

index

about the author

Lisa Kentgen, PhD, is an author and psychologist who has worked in private practice and in academic and research settings. She has presented widely on topics such as living with greater intentionality and treating anxiety and depression. Her writing for scientific publications has covered topics including the development of conscious awareness, the neurobiology of depression and anxiety, and identifying emotional difficulties in children. Seeing an acute need for accessible tools to help us cultivate environments that foster our collective well-being, Kentgen began the research for this book with a focus on communities. She is also the author of *An Intentional Life: Five Foundations of Authenticity and Purpose*. Visit her online at https://the3csofbelonging.substack.com.